CARBON PRICING AND FOSSIL FUEL SUBSIDY RATIONALIZATION TOOL KIT

Rachael Jonassen, Mikael Skou Andersen, Jacqueline Cottrell, and Sandeep Bhattacharya

JULY 2023

ASIAN DEVELOPMENT BANK

ADB

CONTENTS

TABLES, FIGURES, AND BOXES

BOXES

FOREWORD

The coronavirus disease (COVID-19) pandemic, the Russian invasion of Ukraine, and consequent global supply issues have magnified the gap between the financing needed to achieve the Sustainable Development Goals and available resources, which could widen by 70% from before the pandemic. However, the existence of economic crises does not alter the basic climate challenge or the proper response to it. Even a prolonged global recession would have only a modest impact on the stock of atmospheric greenhouse gas emissions. Raising the cost of emissions remains central to addressing the externality problem at the heart of climate change. The policy action required also remains ambitious. Containing global warming to 2°C or less, for example, would require rapidly implementing a global price of at least $75 per ton of carbon dioxide equivalent by 2030, or a dozen times the current global average of $6 per ton. Even if this is achieved, it still may not guarantee achieving the climate targets unless supported by other containment measures.

In general, Asia and the Pacific has a long track record of using environmental taxes—including excise, sales, and import taxes on fossil fuels and other carbon-intensive products—to mobilize general revenue. This ranges from countries that do not impose any environmental tax to Solomon Islands, where environmental taxes contributed 5.4% of gross domestic product in 2019. Apart from Solomon Islands, countries with the highest revenue generated from environmental taxes in the region are Mongolia at 1.7% of gross domestic product, and Japan, New Zealand, and Fiji at 1.3%.[1] The relationship between carbon pricing and environmental taxes is important as they overlap and complement each other, and experience with environmental taxes can be used to implement carbon taxation strategically. In addition, Kazakhstan, New Zealand, the People's Republic of China, and the Republic of Korea implement national emission trading systems, with the Republic of Korea being the first country in East Asia to implement a nationwide mandatory emission trading scheme.

A harmonized climate policy architecture should ensure that carbon pricing is implemented in tandem with the removal or phasing out of fossil fuel subsidies. The International Energy Agency estimates that, among the 25 countries dispensing the most in fossil fuel subsidies in 2020, nine are Asian Development Bank (ADB) developing member countries (DMCs).[2] This indicates that removing existing monetary or financial subsidies for carbon-intensive products such as fossil fuels where they exist should be complementary to imposing a carbon tax.

The main issue for many DMCs contemplating carbon pricing and/or phasing out fossil fuel subsidies is answering the "how" question: How can DMCs design and adopt a viable strategy to combat climate change by using carbon pricing, including subsidy reform, and in the process perhaps generate revenue and improve equity in energy access and use?

---

[1]   Asian Development Bank. 2021. *Carbon Pricing for Green Recovery and Growth*. Manila.

[2]   International Energy Agency. 2022. *Energy Subsidies*. https://www.iea.org/topics/energy-subsidies.

To help DMCs answer this question, ADB has developed this tool kit and road map, which outlines the key steps, challenges, and relevant country experiences for all three elements of getting carbon prices right. Drawing on existing research and knowledge products, this policy brief will help policymakers in ADB DMCs appreciate the landscape and, more importantly, the interplay of carbon pricing instruments and fossil fuel subsidies, as well as understand how these policies synergize or conflict with each other and broader environmental goals. The brief provides step-by-step guidelines to ADB DMCs on how to implement carbon pricing policies for a more effective climate policy mix that is responsive to national circumstances, including climate targets articulated under their respective nationally determined contributions. We hope that this tool kit and ADB assistance based on its key messages will help DMCs achieve their climate ambitions and green, inclusive, and resilient recovery.

Hiranya Mukhopadhyay
Chief, Governance Thematic Group
Sustainable Development and
Climate Change Department
Asian Development Bank

Bruno Carrasco
Director General, Sustainable Development
and Climate Change Department and
concurrently Chief Compliance Officer
Asian Development Bank

ABOUT THE AUTHORS

Rachael Jonassen
Director, Climate Change and Greenhouse Gas Management
Environmental and Energy Management Institute
George Washington University, United States

Rachael Jonassen directs the climate and greenhouse gas management program in the Environmental and Energy Management Institute at George Washington University, where she holds joint appointments in engineering and urban sustainability. She has worked on climate change issues for over 4 decades on issues ranging from high-level nuclear waste disposal, hydroelectric vulnerability, urban adaptation, and mitigation to energy system risks. Her previous positions include managing carbon cycle research at the National Science Foundation and the United States Global Change Research Program; advising the Government of the United States on climate change issues; and international work with the World Bank, United Nations, and Asian Development Bank (ADB). With the World Bank Carbon Pricing Leadership Coalition, she helped organize the first international research meeting on carbon pricing. Rachael holds a doctor of philosophy (PhD) and master of science degrees in geoscience with a research focus on computer simulation.

Mikael Skou Andersen
Professor, cand.scient.pol., PhD
Department of Environmental Science, Aarhus University, Denmark

Mikael Skou Andersen is a full professor of environmental policy analysis at Aarhus University in Denmark, from which he obtained his PhD while a visiting scholar to the Science Center Berlin. He is a member and vice chair of the Scientific Committee of the European Environment Agency. Mikael is the author of *Governance by Green Taxes* (1994) and has researched carbon pricing for more than 25 years. He is coeditor of the *Handbook of Research on Environmental Taxation* (2012) and *Carbon-Energy Taxation: Lessons from Europe* (2009).

Mikael was a member of the expert committee on carbon dioxide taxation to Denmark's Ministry of Taxation and the international task force of the Council for International Cooperation on Environment and Development, advising the People's Republic of China on energy taxation.

Mikael has contributed to numerous reports for international organizations, including *Green Taxation and Other Economic Instruments* (European Commission 2021) and *Green Fiscal Reforms—Strengthening Inclusion and Facilitating the Green Transition* (World Bank 2022). He was principal investigator of the recent Nordic Cooperation-funded project, New Nordic Ways to Green Growth—Strengthening the Foundation for Technological Green Growth Innovation Policy. He is co-organizer of the annual Global Conference on Environmental Taxation.

Jacqueline Cottrell
Green Fiscal Policy Consultant, Freelance Associate
Green Budget Germany

Jacqueline Cottrell is a specialist in green fiscal policy and greening of public financial management, reform of environmentally harmful subsidies, and green budgeting; and a freelance associate of the Berlin-based think tank Green Budget Germany. Since 2004, she has been a self-employed fiscal policy consultant, delivering policy and strategic advisory, human capacity development, and research.

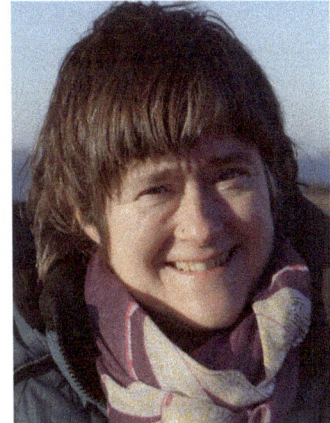

Jacqueline collaborates with a wide range of international organizations, including Deutsche Gesellschaft für Internationale Zusammenarbeit, Agence Française de Développement, Expertise France, the European Commission, United Nations Environment Programme, United Nations Economic and Social Commission for Asia and the Pacific, United Nations Office for Sustainable Development, United Nations Institute for Training and Research, ADB, African Tax Administration Forum, ADB Institute, and Green Budget Germany/Europe. She has published widely in the fields of environmental economics, including on the rationalization of environmentally harmful subsidies.

Sandeep Bhattacharya
Senior Public Management Specialist (Tax), ADB

Sandeep Bhattacharya is a senior specialist in ADB, where he focuses on domestic tax policy initiatives and managing the Secretariat of ADB's Asia Pacific Tax Hub. Sandeep has over 25 years of experience in tax policy and administration, consulting, and academia. Prior to joining ADB, he taught classes in taxation, public economics, statistics, and econometrics, as well as supervised student research at Duke University. He has also worked for close to a decade in tax and customs administration. He has a PhD in economics from Georgia State University and has degrees from Duke University (master of public policy); Delhi School of Economics (master of arts in economics); and St. Stephen's College, Delhi University (bachelor of arts honors in economics).

ACKNOWLEDGMENTS

The development of this tool kit was led by Sandeep Bhattacharya, senior public management specialist (tax), Asian Development Bank, and the chapters were written by Rachael Jonassen, Mikael Skou Andersen, Jacqueline Cottrell, and Sandeep Bhattacharya. The authors would like to thank Bruno Carrasco, director general and concurrently chief compliance officer, Sustainable Development and Climate Change Department (SDCC) and Hiranya Mukhopadhyay, chief of the Governance Thematic Group, for providing strategic guidance, comments, and constant encouragement in the development of this document; and Declan Magee, principal economist, SDCC, who served as the peer reviewer and provided very useful comments to guide the development of the draft tool kit.

ABBREVIATIONS

ADB	Asian Development Bank
CBAM	Carbon Border Adjustment Mechanism
CO_2	carbon dioxide
DMC	developing member country
ETS	emission trading system
EU	European Union
FFS	fossil fuel subsidy
FFSR	fossil fuel subsidy rationalization
GHG	greenhouse gas
ICAP	International Carbon Action Partnership
IEA	International Energy Agency
IMF	International Monetary Fund
LPG	liquefied petroleum gas
NDC	nationally determined contribution
OECD	Organisation for Economic Co-operation and Development
PA	Paris Agreement
PRC	People's Republic of China
RGGI	Regional Greenhouse Gas Initiative
tCO_2e	ton of carbon dioxide equivalent
UNFCCC	United Nations Framework Convention on Climate Change

EXECUTIVE SUMMARY

Emissions of carbon dioxide (CO_2) from the burning of fossil fuels along with other greenhouse gases are causing dangerous changes in the global climate as the average temperatures are increasing everywhere. Recent climate disasters around the world underlie the urgent need to rapidly reduce emissions, as agreed by nations with the 2015 Paris Agreement.

The Asia and Pacific region has seen its emissions increase considerably over the past 2 decades, with numerous countries (developing member countries [DMCs] as well as non-DMCs) now matching or even exceeding the European Union and the United States in per capita emissions. Countries must rapidly reduce greenhouse gas (GHG) emissions to satisfy their nationally determined contributions (NDCs) under the United Nations Framework Convention on Climate Change (UNFCCC) or Paris Agreement. One method to help achieve this objective is an emission trading system (ETS). Leveraging the market, an ETS is a powerful method to curb GHG emissions if the emission cap is stringent. As countries work to achieve their NDCs, they should consider an ETS as a competitive strategy. But developing an ETS can be complicated. The first step lies in the country's determination that an ETS is an appropriate approach to GHG emission reductions for its context.

If a country decides an ETS is the best way to achieve reductions, the Asian Development Bank (ADB), the International Carbon Action Partnership, and the World Bank all have resources to support ADB DMCs' ambitions around ETSs, including step-by-step guides. Although they can be iterative and the order of actions may vary, there are essentially 10 key steps:

(i)   Prepare
(ii)   Decide the Scope
(iii)   Engage Stakeholders, Communicate, and Build Capacity
(iv)   Set the Cap and Compliance Period
(v)   Distribute Allowances
(vi)   Promote a Robust Market
(vii)   Ensure Compliance and Oversight
(viii) Incorporate Flexibilities
(ix)   Consider Linking
(x)   Implement, Evaluate, and Improve

Before designing such a system, the country must establish a legal framework, identify clear objectives, decide the level of formalization and centralization, define core institutional functions, and determine key milestones and timelines for the rollout. Then, they can design the ETS.

Benefits of an ETS to the country include generating revenue; future potential for linkage; complementing other carbon pricing instruments; providing flexibility; design potential to support phased emissions reductions goals; and the flexibility to scale for national, subnational, or sector coverage.

As with most complex economic tools, there is no one-size-fits-all solution. Therefore, policymakers should be careful to consider their countries' unique circumstances and needs. Following implementation, there can be economic, political, and capacity challenges requiring constant reevaluation for a successful ETS.

To keep the average global temperature from exceeding 1.5°C to 2°C, other policy instruments are needed. Carbon taxation is an essential tool in any policy portfolio of measures and instruments to tackle global warming. Experiences from Organisation for Economic Co-operation and Development countries with carbon taxes show the significance of providing unambiguous price signals to all market actors on the need to decarbonize, by gradually increasing taxation or pricing of carbon and its greenhouse equivalents.

Studies from the International Monetary Fund suggest that a carbon tax rate of $25 per ton CO_2 is typically the approximate level to aim for by 2030 to curb emissions in emerging and developing economies, although ultimately, the rate DMC governments choose to impose will depend on the specific socioeconomic, fiscal, and environmental context. At this $25 rate, the price of using coal—the most carbon-intensive of all fuels—is likely to increase by about 50%. Other fuels and gases will also become more expensive, providing low-carbon energy improved leverage in the market.

Unlike an increase in the market prices of energy, revenues from a carbon tax will remain in the domestic economy. The revenues generated will be substantial and can be used to lower other taxes on business and households. A smaller share could be devoted to support low-income households and low-carbon energy technologies, as opted for with Singapore's carbon tax. Advanced economies may have to aim for tax rates of $75 or more by 2030.

Many countries combine carbon taxes with ETSs for the largest emitters of carbon dioxide (power plants and industry). Smaller businesses, households, and transport fuels, on the other hand, are more easily addressed with a carbon tax. Uruguay has recently transformed its excise taxes on motor fuels into a carbon tax. Many countries in Asia and the Pacific have excise taxes on fuels that could be adjusted and extended into a more comprehensive carbon tax. Moreover, only an explicit carbon price will be credited for exports into the European Union, where carbon emissions certificates must be purchased for certain carbon-intensive goods (such as steel and aluminum) from 2026.

The 10 elements of the step-by-step guide to address the process of preparing and introducing a carbon tax are as follows:

(i)   identify the mitigation gap and priority sectors,

(ii)   identify GHGs to be included in tax base,

(iii)   assess implications for specific fuels and risks of carbon leakage,

(iv)   assess distributional impacts,

(v)   calibrate carbon tax rate,

(vi)   determine scope for reductions or exemptions,

(vii)   determine compensations to low-income households,

(viii) assess macroeconomic impacts,

(ix)   determine institutional oversight, and

(x)   establish monitoring for ex-post evaluation.

The theoretical benefits of fossil fuel subsidy rationalization (FFSR) are well-known. Yet in practice, governments encounter a wide range of political economy obstacles when attempting to reform fossil fuel subsidies (FFSs). These often manifest in strong opposition from key interest groups in the extractive, power- and energy-intensive manufacturing sectors, and in protests sparked by concerns about negative social equity impacts. To address these obstacles effectively, governments must take a strategic approach and build a broad political and societal consensus in favor of rationalization within government, across key stakeholders, and among the general populace. The preferred approach emphasizes the importance of a whole-economy approach to FFSR, and the need for careful consideration of potential adverse effects, particularly on distribution and competitiveness.

The approach to FFSR in the guide describes how to prepare the ground for rationalization and is divided into six clearly defined sequential analytical steps. Completing the tasks described at each stage of the process will support DMC governments to develop a clear and robust evidence base upon which to build a strategic plan for rationalization that is politically feasible and thus can be sustained over the long term.

Step 1 provides guidance on how to draw up a subsidy inventory, looking at all necessary steps to build an inventory and quantify subsidies. Step 2 explains how DMC governments can go about understanding the ways in which subsidies influence fossil fuel prices and how the mechanisms underlying subsidies work, who subsidies benefit, and how. Step 3 describes a range of qualitative and quantitative approaches policymakers can use to predict the impacts of FFSR, from literature reviews, checklists, and conceptual mapping through to input–output models and econometric modeling. The final preparatory step, Step 4, draws together the analysis and highlights key considerations when drawing up a priority list of FFSs for rationalization.

The ranking and analysis derived from the preparatory phase should feed into and inform the development of a long-term subsidy rationalization strategy, tailored to the specific DMC context and designed with the permanent rationalization of FFSs in mind. Therefore, Step 5 is an in-depth strategic design phase which focuses on three major elements: institution building, time frame, and communication and consensus building. Finally, once one or more elements of FFSR have been implemented, Step 6 looks at monitoring and adjustment of policy measures.

The introduction of carbon pricing—whether in the form of an ETS, carbon taxation, or the removal of negative carbon prices through FFSR—is a challenging and politically sensitive process. Low carbon prices are deeply embedded in the economies and fiscal systems of many countries. Nevertheless, DMC governments will need to rationalize FFSs and introduce carbon pricing to deliver on their NDCs and achieve the Sustainable Development Goals of the Agenda 2030. This guide breaks down this process into a series of logical steps, and it is hoped that this will serve as an important enabler of FFSR and the introduction of carbon pricing in ADB DMCs in the future.

1 INTRODUCTION

The Asia and Pacific region remains especially vulnerable to the negative impacts of climate change on livelihoods, food and water security, and public health. In 2019, about 50% of global carbon dioxide (CO_2) emissions from fossil fuel combustion originated from the region. Therefore, it can be asserted that the battle against climate change will be won or lost in Asia and the Pacific. As the region's climate bank, the Asian Development Bank (ADB) is committed to supporting its developing member countries (DMCs) tackle climate change, build climate and disaster resilience, and enhance environmental sustainability. This is also an operational priority under ADB's Strategy 2030.

The transition to clean, reliable, and affordable energy while ensuring energy access for all is key to achieving the region's climate objectives. As part of ADB's efforts to foster the energy transition, ADB is working with regional and international partners to pilot a scalable energy transition mechanism, which is a collaborative initiative developed in partnership with the bank's DMCs that will leverage a market-based approach to accelerate the transition from fossil fuels to clean energy.

ADB recognizes that the region's energy financing needs far exceed the resources of any single actor. Further climate finance is needed alongside a comprehensive and effective climate policy mix with the appropriate policy instruments to meet energy transition needs and targets under the Paris Agreement. Carbon pricing can be a key element of the broader climate policy architecture that can help countries reduce greenhouse gas (GHG) emissions cost-effectively, and foster energy transition and decarbonization.

Carbon pricing is a climate policy approach used in several countries and subnational jurisdictions around the world. Carbon pricing works by charging emitters for the emissions of CO_2 for which they are responsible. Carbon pricing policies traditionally take two forms: carbon taxes and cap-and-trade programs. A harmonized climate policy should ensure that carbon pricing is implemented alongside the reduction or phasing out of fossil fuel subsidies (FFSs), which work like negative carbon taxes because they lower the price of fossil fuels. Carbon pricing can incentivize investments in low-carbon technologies and help countries achieve the targets set out in their nationally determined contributions (NDCs) cost-effectively and generate revenue that can be channeled toward climate-related or other development initiatives.

ADB has a long-standing engagement in this area, mobilizing carbon finance through the Asia Pacific Carbon Fund, the Future Carbon Fund, and the Japan Fund for the Joint Crediting Mechanism. ADB has also been providing technical support through its Technical Support Facility and the Article 6 Support Facility to support its DMCs to take advantage of various carbon pricing instruments. ADB will continue to take a holistic approach to carbon pricing and markets by mobilizing carbon finance, incentivizing investments in low-carbon technologies, and providing technical and capacity-building support to its DMCs.

The Asia Pacific Tax Hub, housed within the Governance Thematic Group of ADB's Sustainable Development and Climate Change Department, developed this tool kit to facilitate dialogue within ADB DMCs and help government officials design and implement carbon pricing programs. While more detailed manuals exist on each of the three components considered (emission trading system [ETS], taxes, and fossil fuel subsidy rationalization [FFSR]), it was felt that a succinct and compact "how to" tool kit that summarized the relevant practical guidance in one document would be useful to those charged with designing and implementing carbon pricing policies. The interested reader intent on digging deeper into any one of the topics discussed in this manual can also benefit from pursuing the references and sources cited in this document.

One method to curb GHG emissions and prevent dangerous climate change is to establish an ETS. An ETS puts a cap on emissions and allows participating entities to trade allowances, creating a market that rewards lower emissions, incentivizes innovation for greater efficiency, and perhaps generates revenue. ADB offers multiple lines of support to its DMCs that wish to implement an ETS.

In Chapter 2 of this document, Rachael Jonassen provides a step-by-step guide on how to create and implement an ETS. It is intended to help policymakers in ADB DMCs consider the best methods and systems for emission reductions to meet their NDC under the United Nations Framework Convention on Climate Change (Paris Agreement). Such policymakers can be in environment ministries, or be lawmakers, prime ministers, and even presidents. Although emphasizing national policy and implementation, case studies at the regional and subnational scale are included to demonstrate best practices and the strategic benefits of starting with a scaled-down system.

This document explains what an ETS is and how to develop a national system. It assumes that a country has determined that an ETS is appropriate for its context. It explains the importance of establishing a legal framework and outlines how to decide key objectives, the appropriate level of formalization, and core institutional functions. It explains how to measure progress and when to reevaluate.

The Design the System section of Chapter 2 lays out 10 steps to create and implement an ETS. The steps outlined here draw from earlier compendia on ETS development methodologies prepared by the International Carbon Action Partnership and the World Bank, as well as case studies that illustrate best practices and lessons learned from existing ETSs and those under development across ADB DMCs. Finally, this report describes economic, political, and capacity challenges policymakers face in implementing such a strategy and how to address them, as well as where to find support and resources for ETS implementation.

Most observers consider carbon taxation indispensable, to complement an ETS or a broader policy portfolio. A carbon tax puts a price on emissions of CO_2 and other GHGs, allowing emitters more flexibility than under command-and-control regulations. A carbon tax generates revenue which can be used to lower other taxes, directly compensate low-income households, or further the adoption of low-carbon technology.

In Chapter 3 of this tool kit, Mikael Skou Andersen provides, in a concise guide, insights on the issues associated with introducing national carbon taxation and offers step-by-step guidance on how to design and implement these taxes. It includes case material illustrating practices and experiences with carbon taxation from emerging economies around the world and an extensive list of references for further reading.

Governments encounter a wide range of political obstacles when attempting to reform FFSs, despite the well-known benefits of FFSR. To address these obstacles effectively, governments must take a strategic approach to FFSR and build a broad political and societal consensus in favor of rationalization.

In Chapter 4, Jacqueline Cottrell offers a step-by-step guide that unpacks the FFSR process and explains key considerations and analytical requirements of each stage, from preparing the ground and drawing up an inventory of FFSs to designing a rationalization strategy and monitoring its implementation. It has been developed for policymakers and ministry staff in ADB DMCs and examines all the major political questions that must be addressed for FFSR to be successful and sustained over the long term.

There are many issues that have not been elaborated on, further keeping in mind the purpose of this tool kit. For example, voluntary carbon markets have not been discussed explicitly as we decided to focus on ones that would be set up and regulated by policymakers. By explicit choice, we have chosen to eschew posing any country system as a "model" or an example to follow for other DMCs. Instead, we chose to offer examples of what other countries have done in areas where DMCs will have to make choices. Rather than prescribing to the reader the "best practice" to follow, the authors have presented different approaches that other countries have adopted.

Finally, the reader may have already recognized that the three components are not separate from each other as all three policies seek to raise the price of carbon. The natural questions that follow are the correct choice of the policy mix and the agencies that may need to get involved in implementation.

A. Introduction

All countries must reduce greenhouse gas (GHG) emissions to satisfy their nationally determined contribution (NDC) under the United Nations Framework Convention on Climate Change (UNFCCC) and its ratified Paris Agreement. Emission trading systems (ETSs) have helped many governments (Box 1) address their commitments using efficient financial incentives in a decentralized market system (Di Maria, Zarkovic, and Hintermann 2020; PMR and ICAP 2022). Eighteen developing member countries (DMCs) of the Asian Development Bank (ADB) reference ETSs in their NDCs for GHG reduction, six of them intending to sell carbon credits to other countries.

Box 1

Emission Trading Systems to Date

With nearly 2 decades of experience, carbon emission trading systems continue to grow in scope.

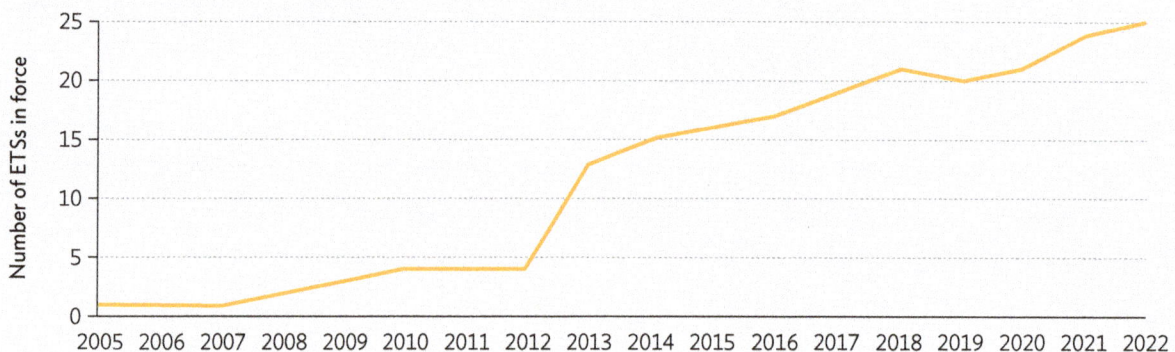

ETSs = emission trading systems.

Notes: As of 2022, 25 ETSs in the European Union and eight other countries, and 25 in subnational jurisdictions, regulate 17% of global greenhouse gas emissions and have produced a cumulative $161 billion in revenue. Another 22 ETSs are under preparation.

Source: International Carbon Action Partnership. 2022a. *Emissions Trading Worldwide: Status Report 2022*. Berlin. https://icapcarbonaction.com/system/files/document/220408_icap_report_exsum_en.pdf.

An ETS aims to decrease investment in high-emission activities and increase investment in clean energy technology. As laid out in Article 6 of the Paris Agreement (Box 2), an ETS can generate public revenue to invest in complementary activities or address adverse impacts (IEA 2020). As efficient and effective as ETSs are, various design features affect success (Haites 2018; Mirzaee Ghazani and Ali Jafari 2021). This guide is intended to help the ADB DMCs design effective ETSs.

Box 2

New Opportunities under Article 6

Article 6 of the Paris Agreement establishes a framework for international cooperation in carbon markets.

Article 6.2 allows purchased mitigation units, called internationally transferred mitigation outcomes (ITMOs), to apply toward nationally determined commitments and their sale to secure funding. Countries can link their emission trading system (ETS) with another country under the Article 6.2 mechanism.

Article 6.4 provides rules for a global trading system under the Paris Agreement and encourages countries to cancel ITMOs for overall mitigation in global emissions.

Countries should consider the Article 6 mechanism as they design an ETS. The regulatory and accounting systems of an ETS can address the accounting requirements for trading ITMOs, which can fund climate action.

Source: Asian Development Bank.

A cap-and-trade ETS (Figure 1) sets an overall emission limit or cap, which is normally lowered over time in line with a country's emission reduction goals.[1] Within the cap, tradable emission allowances are allocated—to the various sectors, activities, and/or geographic areas that are required to participate— by auction, free allocation, or a combination of the two (ADB 2016a). As free allocations are reduced, entities stay within their cap by reducing emissions and/or purchasing allowances and/or offset credits, considering relative costs.

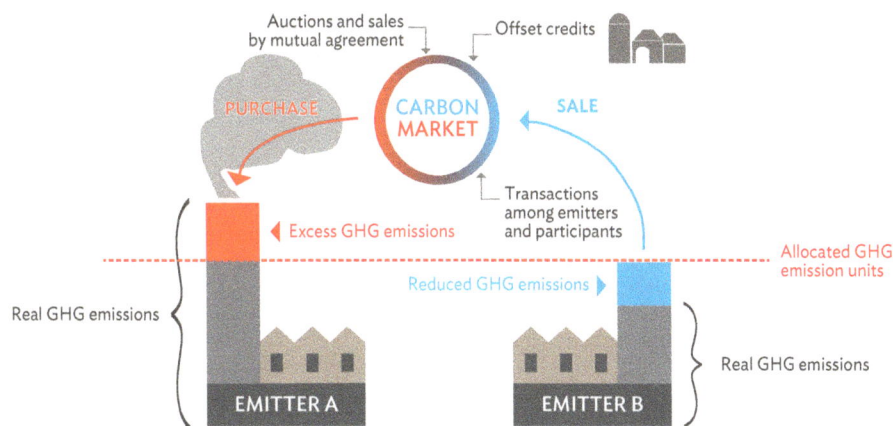

Figure 1: A Cap-and-Trade System Creates a Carbon Market to Efficiently Drive Emission Reduction

GHG = greenhouse gas.
Source: Government of Ontario, Ministry of Environment and Climate Change.
https://cleanenergycanada.org/ontarios-first-cap-trade-auction-best-viewed-wide-angle-lens/.

---

[1]   The structure of an ETS can be customized. Indonesia's planned ETS, for example, will be a cap-trade-and-tax system, subjecting entities that exceed their emissions cap to a carbon tax (ICAP 2022b).

The following sections discuss how to establish a legal framework for an ETS and design the system.

B. Establish a Legal Framework

Since a mandatory ETS necessarily limits the economic freedom of covered entities, it is important to have a clear legal basis that (i) codifies the authority of the government to implement such a system, and (ii) lays out the rights and obligations of participants. By codifying the ETS in law, the system gains legitimacy and greater political durability, allowing the ETS to send a price signal that encourages the private sector to invest appropriately, setting the stage for a more effective system (PMR and ICAP 2022). If an ETS is not yet included as part of a country's NDC, including it in the next NDC update signals the country's political commitment.

1. Clearly identify objectives.

In the early stages of planning, a DMC should define the role of the ETS in a policy package.[2] The package may include the following:

(i)   incentivizing private sector adoption of cleaner technology through revenue reinvested in research and development;

(ii)   reinforcing existing regulations and standards;[3]

(iii) supporting a climate justice agenda whereby revenue is used to offset negative economic effects or to support the climate resilience of vulnerable populations; and

(iv)   enjoying the co-benefits of emission reductions such as reduced air pollution, improved public health, and increased energy security (Eden et al. 2018).

Box 3

Case Study: Defining Objectives for Viet Nam

In January 2022, the revised Law on Environmental Protection legalized the establishment of a carbon market with four complementary objectives:

- reducing air pollution to protect human health,
- reducing climate change impacts and environmental degradation,
- raising revenue to encourage innovation and greener technologies, and
- attracting greater foreign direct investment and increasing export competitiveness.

Viet Nam's goals demonstrate how emission trading systems are uniquely able to achieve disparate objectives through a single mechanism.

Source: World Bank. 2022. *State and Trends of Carbon Pricing*.

Objectives must align with commitments in the NDC. Other practices, such as using revenue to support ETS goals, should be included in framework legislation (Box 3). An ETS may be wrapped with complementary policies in the same legal document, which is often an amendment to an existing climate or environmental law.

---

2   "Such complementary policies could include the introduction of performance standards; new rules for city design, land and forest management, and investments in infrastructure; the development of new methods and technologies; and the use of financial instruments that foster private sector participation and reduce the risk-weighted capital costs of low-carbon technologies and projects" (High-Level Commission on Carbon Prices 2017).

3   To reduce emissions, California has adopted several measures: a renewables portfolio standard, a low-carbon fuel standard, vehicle emission standards, and energy efficiency measures. If these measures do not meet emissions reduction goals, an ETS offers a backstop (IEA, n.d.).

2. Determine the level of formalization and centralization.

Framework legislation should reflect the level of formalization desired. More formal systems, which write into the legislation greater detail about design and implementation, tend to be more stable and legitimate, and thus are better able to guide stakeholder expectations. The formality of the European Union (EU) ETS, for example, has allowed it to withstand numerous legal challenges. However, formalization limits a system's agility, such that it took 5 years for the EU ETS to adopt new flexibility measures in response to the 2009 financial crisis (PMR and ICAP 2022). Less formalized systems are easier to adopt and allow more flexibility throughout planning and implementation.

Legislation may authorize only a national ETS or else subnational systems as well. Seven subnational pilots are part of ETS design in the People's Republic of China (PRC). Key decisions regarding the level of government decision-making can also be legislated. The Regional Greenhouse Gas Initiative (RGGI) in the eastern United States is coordinated regionally but regulated by states. States seeking to join the RGGI are required to adopt regulations that align with the established RGGI Model Rule; states thus have their individual legal mandates, but alignment across all participating states allows efficient collaboration in the regional ETS (RGGI 2022).

3. Define core institutional functions.

The diverse functions associated with setting up and implementing an ETS call for clarity among responsible entities. An administrator managing day-to-day operations may be a new entity created under framework legislation. The lead ministry under which the administrator functions should be identified, as should the duties of other ministries. As compliance enforcement, market oversight, and regulation are sensitive functions critical to a well-functioning ETS, government institutions must have a clear mandate for these roles. Legislation may also set forth procedures for the design, implementation, monitoring, and review of the system and indicate who has authority to make key decisions regarding the ETS, such as how and when the cap will be set and revised, and how sectors will be selected.

4. Identify key milestones and timelines for rollout.

Framework legislation should include an overall vision, a timeline for rollout, and parameters for further planning and implementation. The legislation may require environmental, economic, regulatory, and/or social impact analyses. It may require a pilot phase. Such directives galvanize stakeholders, both internal and external. An ambitious but feasible timeline for rollout provides a strong signal that emission reduction is required, which helps private firms make investment decisions for cleaner technology before implementation.

C. Design the System

Once the legal framework is in place, policymakers can embark on designing the ETS through a 10-step process (Figure 2). While the steps are presented sequentially, many systems require parallel efforts and iteration, and experts do not agree on the best order of these steps. It is better to think of them as a set of supporting actions, all of which help create a successful ETS.

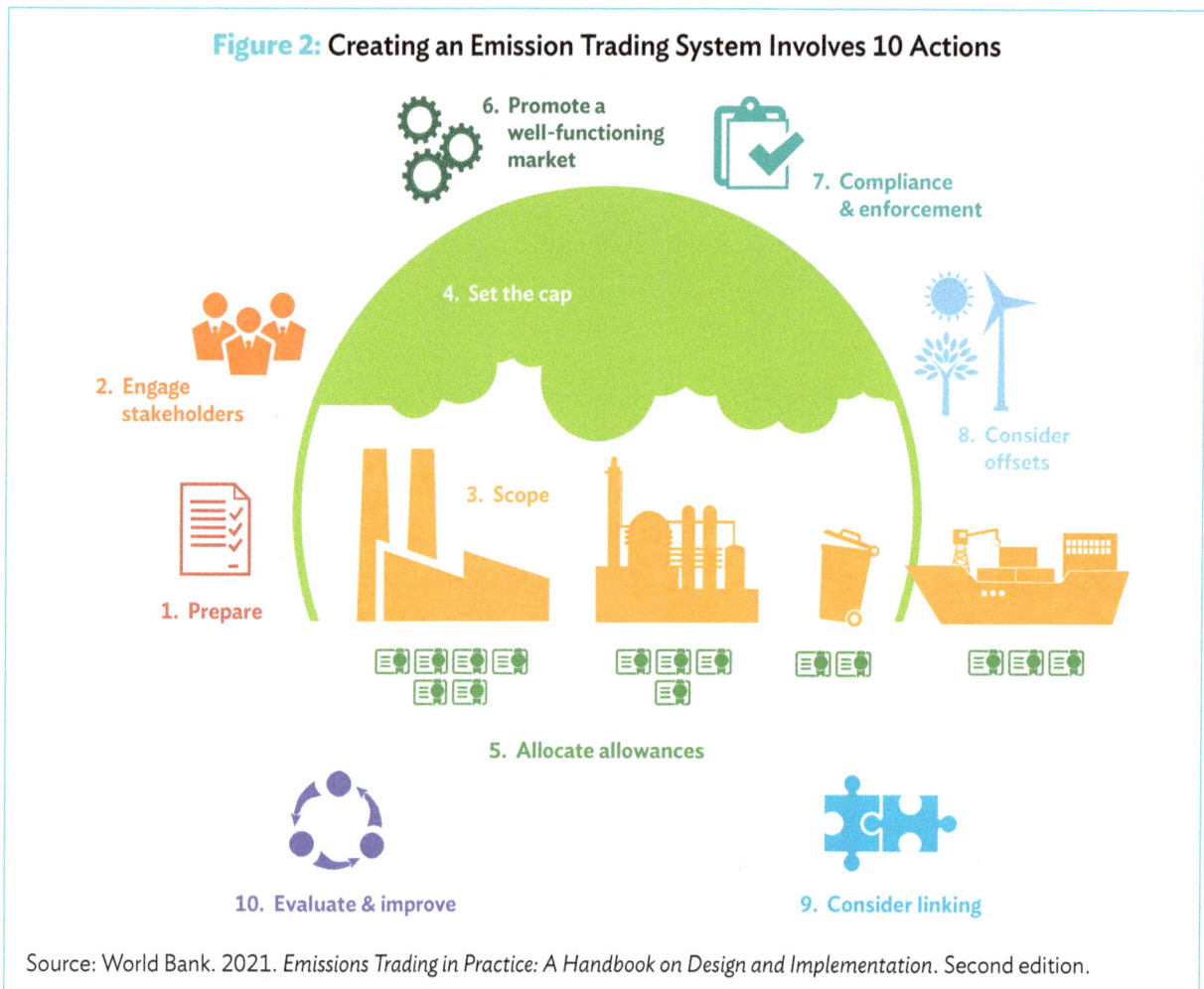

Figure 2: Creating an Emission Trading System Involves 10 Actions

6. Promote a well-functioning market

7. Compliance & enforcement

4. Set the cap

2. Engage stakeholders

8. Consider offsets

3. Scope

1. Prepare

5. Allocate allowances

10. Evaluate & improve

9. Consider linking

Source: World Bank. 2021. *Emissions Trading in Practice: A Handbook on Design and Implementation*. Second edition.

1. Prepare.

Emissions must be measured reliably to identify key sectors and sources to include in the ETS and to design appropriate reduction strategies (Box 4). Countries that have submitted national inventory reports to the UNFCCC, as part of biennial update reports by non-Annex 1 Parties, already have a clear idea which sectors are the major sources of carbon emissions in their country (UN Climate Change[a], n.d.). These reports can form the basis for determining sectors to consider for inclusion in the ETS and when to incorporate additional sectors.

Each major emitter should report emissions in tons of carbon dioxide equivalent (tCO_2e). Reporting makes clear which entities will be covered under the ETS and builds entity capacity for the reporting process. It may take a few years to fully develop expertise within covered entities and the regulatory authority to correctly measure, report, and verify emissions. Before and during that time, the regulatory authority must set the reporting framework, which may include online reporting tools and training. Once a covered entity can consistently and reliably report emissions, its reports should undergo third-party verification, which may be iterative.

Box 4

Case Study: Baseline in India

The Surat pilot developed a baseline using a continuous emission monitoring system to highlight which sectors, activities, and gases should be prioritized. Continuous emission monitoring system data prioritized particulate matter emissions (PM2.5) from gas and industrial emissions. The Surat baseline informed setting a cap and distributing allowances.

Reductions from participating industries were compared to those of business-as-usual industries to gauge the effectiveness of the emission trading system.

Baselines serve multiple purposes.

Source: IndiaSpend. *Explained: How Surat's Emissions Trading Scheme Works to Reduce Air Pollution.* https://www.indiaspend.com/explainers/surat-emission-trading-scheme-gujarat-works-to-reduce-air-pollution-763554.

A well-developed, consistent, and verified record establishes the base year value of emissions. Reductions are measured from the base year, setting a cap in a cap-and-trade system, which may become the emission allowance issued to the covered entity when the ETS begins. A well-functioning reporting process allows the regulatory authority and covered entity to properly track reductions. Entity-level reports help the country track its progress in reducing emissions in the ETS as part of its UNFCCC report.

Understanding base year emissions and the processes that produce them allows emissions to be projected assuming no interventions. This projection becomes the baseline. The baseline and record of reductions measure the effectiveness of policy interventions.

2. Decide the scope.

Policymakers should weigh two key factors in adding sectors to the ETS: the quantity of emissions and the number of participants (ADB 2016a). These factors affect the cap and allowances chosen. The broader the range of sectors, activities, and GHGs included under the ETS, the higher the mitigation potential. In addition, markets are more fluid with more participants, and mitigation efforts are likely to be more cost-effective when the largest sectors are included (Box 5). However, a larger pool also increases regulatory load. Because smaller entities have higher relative costs for monitoring, reporting, and verification, ETSs often employ minimum emission thresholds that exclude entities with lower emissions. Similarly, in prioritizing GHGs, policymakers should consider the costs and technical requirements of monitoring, reporting, and verification. Some gases are more difficult to monitor than others.

Best practice is to start with a limited scope and expand as capacity grows. Most systems begin with the electric power sector and then venture into additional sectors as capacity for expansion allows. To date, most emission reductions have been achieved in the power sector, ensuring a larger network of knowledge and research. In the EU ETS, options for additional sectors include heavy industry and aviation (European Commission 2021). However, other key sectors to keep in mind could be building, transportation, waste, and shipping.

Box 5

Case Study: Scope in the People's Republic of China

Seven pilot projects covered the highest emitters in prioritized sectors, activities, and greenhouse gases emitted. They covered 30% of gross domestic product and a significant portion of emissions from the People's Republic of China (PRC). The national emission trading system focused first only on power plants, as base year emissions showed coal-powered power plants accounting for most emissions. From the beginning, the PRC considered adding iron and steel, aluminum, cement, chemicals, papermaking, and civil aviation. As of 2022, the PRC plans to add heavy industry and manufacturing, widening the scope by 70%.

Source: World Bank. 2022. *State and Trends of Carbon Pricing*.

3. Engage stakeholders, communicate, and build capacity.

Because ETSs have broad national impact, they require public and political support. Stakeholder engagement helps secure approval and continued support for ETS policy. Policymakers should identify key stakeholders, such as those in Figure 3, and understand their positions, interests, and concerns regarding an ETS (Box 6).

Figure 3: Four Objectives of Stakeholder Engagement

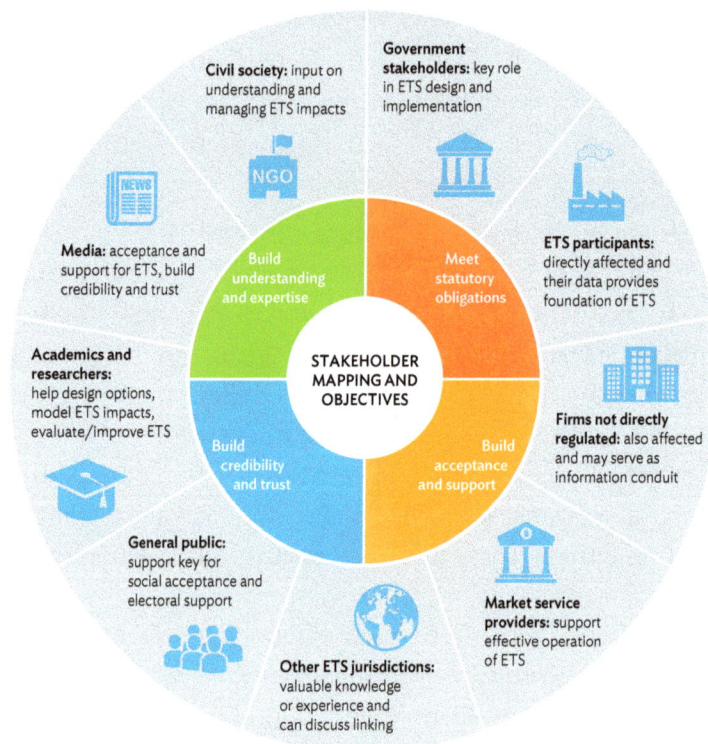

ETS = emission trading system, NGO = nongovernment organization.

Source: ICAP. 2021. ICAP ETS Briefs. Berlin: International Carbon Action Partnership. https://icapcarbonaction.com/en/publications/icap-ets-briefs.

Box 6

Case Study: Engagement in India

Developing economies such as India rely on energy-intensive industries. Emission trading systems (ETSs) for reducing energy use may be a sensitive and controversial topic. India recognized the need for stakeholder engagement to successfully introduce ETS policy. While preparing a national ETS, stakeholder engagement has been a top priority. Stakeholder engagement from an early stage of project planning ensured that the project's feasibility, risks, and impacts were all well considered. Borrowing from the stakeholder engagement plan of the Republic of Korea, India includes ongoing public hearings and consultations from industry leaders.

Learning from other countries with an ETS can ease the total effort.

Source: Government of India, Ministry of Power. *National Carbon Market.* https://beeindia.gov.in/sites/default/files/publications/files/NCM%20Final.pdf.

Policymakers should coordinate across stakeholders to increase transparency while avoiding policy gaps or issues. It may help to designate a policy team member to be the point of contact for stakeholders. Best practice is to design an engagement strategy (PMR and CPLC 2018). This helps ensure that all stakeholders are consulted at each step. Engagement processes should be transparent and include all groups. Equal consideration should also be given to public and private actors to encourage strong public–private collaboration.

Roundtables gather stakeholders to express concerns and viewpoints, making them a great tool for engaging stakeholders. Engagement does not end after policy implementation but extends to regular assessments to ensure that the policy is working as intended. This process can be slow but, if done well, helps ensure broad acceptance of the policy.

Leery stakeholders can be transformed into supporters by building relationships with them, meaningfully including them in design considerations, and demonstrating why an ETS is best for the country as a whole. This makes stakeholder engagement vital early in the process. Building capacity in covered entities ensures that they develop the skills, processes, and tools needed to function properly within the ETS (Box 7).

Box 7

Case Study: Capacity Building in the People's Republic of China

In 2022, the People's Republic of China moved into a new phase largely focused on capacity building. As its emission trading system evolves to use new technologies and include new sectors, its capacity-building program evolves to help stakeholders learn new methods and technologies. The country's emission trading system technical assistance program is the biggest in the world.

Source: World Bank. 2022. *State and Trends of Carbon Pricing.*

Stakeholder engagement and capacity building go hand in hand, as stakeholders must be able to understand, analyze, and respond to ETS policy. However, the capacity required will differ depending upon the stakeholders and their role. To build capacity, policymakers can integrate education, develop guidelines, and offer training to stakeholders and staff. Several educational tools and workshop models already exist. Capacity-building tools should be regularly evaluated to ensure that they achieve set objectives and evolve with the broader ETS policy.

4. Set the cap and compliance period.

Caps and compliance periods are fundamental components of an ETS. The cap is the total amount of emissions—expressed in tCO_2e with each ton referred to as an allowance unit—that will be allowed over a given period, called the compliance period. Over time, the cap is reduced in alignment with the country's GHG emission reduction goals, which should be defined in its NDC and broken down further by sector, activity, and GHG. As the cap is reduced, participants have incentive to seek innovative methods of reducing emissions. With a subnational ETS, good practice is to coordinate its cap with the national goal to prevent accounting errors (Box 8).

Box 8

Case Study: Emission Cap in Japan

Japan's system is useful as a guide to linking several subnational emission trading systems in a way that prevents double counting and carbon leakage. While prefectures have their own systems, the cap and scope are set nationally. Allowances are distributed according to historic emissions.

Be flexible in how caps are determined and applied.

Source: Asian Development Bank. 2016. *Emissions Trading Schemes and Their Linking: Challenges and Opportunities in Asia and the Pacific.* Manila.
https://www.adb.org/sites/default/files/publication/182501/emissions-trading-schemes.pdf.

---

a. Cap-Setting Approach

Data requirements. Policymakers use a range of data to determine the cap ambition and cap type: historical emissions, future emission projections under a baseline scenario, technical and economic ability, potential to reduce emissions, existing policy enablers or barriers to mitigation, and national or sector mitigation goals.

Determining cap ambition. Policymakers need to weigh three issues when setting the cap ambition for the ETS: (i) trade-offs between emission reduction and ETS cost, (ii) alignment of the cap ambition with a wider environmental target, and (iii) the share of responsibility between capped and uncapped sectors (Healy 2018).

Cap type. There are two cap types. Absolute caps fix the allowance amount in advance. Intensity caps issue allowances per unit of input or output, such as tCO_2e per unit of gross domestic product. Intensity caps are possible in theory but difficult in practice when trying to allocate allowances to sectors or firms (Baron 2012).

Approaches. Top–down cap-setting does so with an eye to future emissions based on climate change data, GHG emission objectives in NDCs, costs, or the caps set by comparable countries. Bottom–up cap-setting starts with a firm or sector and can be based on emission intensity. In this approach, emitters that exceed a set level of emissions report production and energy consumption data to local governments, which allocate allowances according to regional or national goals. These firm and sector totals are key data for setting the cap. Policymakers can combine these two strategies (top–down and bottom–up) to set the cap.

b. Cap-Setting Process

The following are the usual steps to setting caps:

(i)   Set national goals and secure political backing.

(ii)   Gather historical emission data, especially at the firm and sector levels.

(iii)   Determine the baseline from which to reduce emissions.

(iv)   Calculate sector emission projections and output for future emission scenarios.

(v)   Determine technical opportunities for reducing emissions and their economic costs.

(vi)   Involve climate change policy groups and sector leaders.

(vii) Consider securing access to domestic or international offsets, linking other ETSs, and banking emission allowances.

Two techniques are used to set a cap: (i) by linear reduction factor and (ii) applying a percentage deviation in emissions from a selected emission projection or baseline (Healy 2018). In Mexico, a cap based on a linear reduction factor follows a projected absolute change in emissions relative to 2016 emissions and then applies that change to each year of the compliance period, for example, a 1% annual reduction in emissions from the 2016 baseline (Figure 4). The second approach aligns the cap to Mexico's NDC business-as-usual baseline in each year of the trading period. In this scenario, Mexico has a target to reduce emissions by 22% from its business-as-usual baseline.

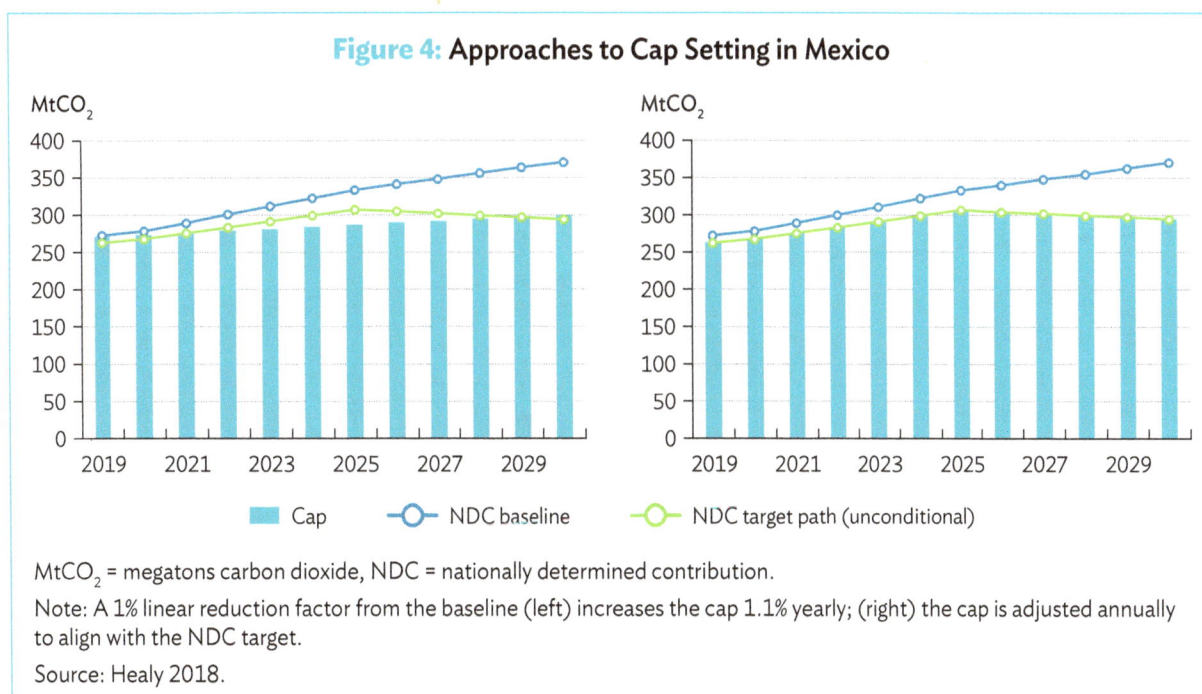

Figure 4: Approaches to Cap Setting in Mexico

$MtCO_2$ = megatons carbon dioxide, NDC = nationally determined contribution.

Note: A 1% linear reduction factor from the baseline (left) increases the cap 1.1% yearly; (right) the cap is adjusted annually to align with the NDC target.

Source: Healy 2018.

In Figure 4, the cap in the linear reduction factor scenario does not align with Mexico's NDC target path but instead follows a 1% increase in annual emissions during the period. The deviation scenario cap directly aligns with the NDC target path.

Most ETSs have a compliance period of 1–5 years (Box 9). Short compliance periods can be challenging because emissions are not always predictable, as illustrated by recent experience during the COVID-19 pandemic.

Box 9

Case Study: Allowances in India

In most cases, as in the Indian city of Surat, the regulatory body oversees both establishing the cap and distributing allowances. The initial compliance period of the Surat emission trading system was very short at only 6 months. Using the grandparenting method, 80% of the credits were distributed for free, and the other 20% were auctioned. Based on their compliance status at the end of a compliance period, participants could trade credits on a carbon market. Following this compliance period, the progress made by each participant was evaluated and allowances for the next compliance period were determined.

The period of compliance can be shorter than 1 year.

Source: IndiaSpend. *Explained: How Surat's Emissions Trading Scheme Works to Reduce Air Pollution.* https://www.indiaspend.com/explainers/surat-emission-trading-scheme-gujarat-works-to-reduce-air-pollution-763554.

Emissions can vary from year to year in line with business decisions or market fluctuations; to smoothen variation, regulatory bodies may choose to set the compliance period as multiple years (Box 10). On the other hand, if compliance periods are too long, covered entities may postpone efforts to reduce emissions, making the ETS less effective in the short term. Regardless of the length of the compliance period, the cap for each period should align with short-term objectives on the path to long-term goals and NDCs.

Box 10

Case Study: Compliance Period and Caps in Kazakhstan

Kazakhstan has set meaningful goals for its emission trading system (ETS), both short term and long term. They include a 15% reduction below 1990 levels by 2025. The country has a goal of being carbon-neutral by 2060[a] and its ETS caps reflect this target.[b] Kazakhstan's ETS operates on 2-year compliance periods, and each year of the compliance period has its own cap. For example, in the 2014–2015 compliance period, the cap for 2014 was 155.4 megatons of carbon dioxide and, for 2015, it was 153 megatons.

[a] J. F. Marteau. 2021. *From Paris to Glasgow and Beyond: Towards Kazakhstan's Carbon Neutrality by 2060.* World Bank. https://blogs.worldbank.org/europeandcentralasia/paris-glasgow-and-beyond-towards-kazakhstans-carbon-neutrality-2060#:~:text=The%20ETS%20began%20in%202013,heating%2C%20extractive%20industries%20and%20manufacturing.

[b] Environmental Defense Fund. 2016. *Kazakhstan: An Emissions Trading Case Study.* https://www.edf.org/sites/default/files/kazakhstan_case_study.pdf.

Yearly compliance reviews can be costly, so the budget should be part of that determination. The length of the compliance period helps determine the use and applicability of offsets and other flexible instruments, which will be discussed in later steps. Other aspects of compliance period planning include determining the carbon price per unit, GHGs and sectors to be covered, number of participants, and compliance tools and flexibilities that are allowed.

The Paris Agreement operates on a 5-year compliance period. Article 9 of the agreement states that every 5 years starting from 2023, all member countries will report progress made toward their NDCs, and a global inventory will be taken. To minimize reporting burdens, countries might consider adopting a complementary compliance period for their ETSs.

5. Distribute allowances.

Allowances fix the amount of emissions each covered entity can release in a compliance period. After establishing the overall cap for the ETS, allowances are distributed among covered entities through either free allocation or auctioning at the start of each compliance period. Free allocation is often used when an ETS is first established to mitigate disruption to regulated sectors and prevent leakage. Because free allocation can undermine carbon market efficiency, countries often shift toward auctioning as the ETS matures (Box 11).

Box 11

Case Study: Allowances in the People's Republic of China

After setting a cap and distributing allowances, the People's Republic of China found that some provinces benefited more than others. Depending on their economic activities, some provinces maintained large surpluses while others suffered large deficits, leaving highly uneven economic impacts. Studies have shown that this could reflect the system of free distribution that the country used. A possible solution is to slowly introduce auctioning.

Expect surprises when introducing and operating emission trading systems.

Source: International Energy Agency. 2020.
https://iea.blob.core.windows.net/assets/d21bfabc-ac8a-4c41-bba7-e792cf29945c/
China_Emissions_Trading_Scheme.pdf.

If free allocation is chosen, the amount allocated to each covered entity can be determined in two ways (ICAP, n.d.):

(i)   **Grandparenting.** Allowances are determined based on historical emissions. A base year or period is established, and allowances are determined based on each entity's historical emissions during that time. For example, if an entity produced 10 tCO_2e during the base period, it would receive 10 allowances for the compliance period.

(ii)   **Benchmarking.** Allowances are calculated based on each entity's production, either historical or based on current output multiplied by a standard emission intensity benchmark (which may be based upon what is possible with improved technology). For example, if the benchmark is set at 0.7 allowances per unit of output and the entity produces 10 units of output during the compliance period, it would receive 7.0 allowances.

Both allocation options offer advantages and disadvantages. Grandparenting is the more expedient politically and economically because it has lower startup costs to governments and companies. On the downside, it can reward higher emitters by designating more allowances and bar entry for smaller participants. Benchmarking has higher startup costs, but it encourages greater efforts and is perhaps more equitable.

It is important to recognize the potential impact of free allocation approaches on firms' entry into the sector, and their exit. Both grandparenting and historical benchmarking can pose barriers to entry because new firms would not receive free allocations. Because it does not rely on historical emissions, output-based free allocation is the best option when new entrants are a primary concern. With regard to closing firms, grandparenting and historical benchmarking can be problematic because closing firms can sell their free allocations for windfall profit. This can be remedied by requiring firms to maintain operations for a minimum period to receive free allocations (PMR and ICAP 2021).

If the system operates by requiring participants to pay for allowances, their price is often determined through an auction. This system helps to raise revenue that can be used to operate the ETS, check compliance, and support other goals such as facilitating adaptation and resilience. Auctions are recommended to prevent collusion and promote transparency by showing demand for allowances (ADB 2016a).

Once allowances are set, participants must abate their emissions or acquire allowances from other participants who do not need all of theirs. A standard feature of an ETS is that participants who have excess allowances can sell their surplus for profit. This is the "trade" component of a cap-and-trade system. Before the end of a compliance period, participants trade on the carbon market as needed to ensure all participants are in compliance, possessing allowances at least equal to their actual emissions.

The idea is to reduce the cap, and therefore allowances, over successive compliance periods, encouraging participants to reduce their emissions rather than rely on purchasing surplus allowances. With a declining cap, such purchases become more costly over time.[4]

6. Promote a well-functioning market.

ETSs have all the advantages, disadvantages, and imperfections of any free market system. Experience globally shows that markets must be regulated to avoid the worst disadvantages of a market while maximizing the advantages.[5] To this end, ETS frameworks have cost containment and emissions containment reserves (Box 12).

The regulatory body holds in a cost containment reserve an agreed number of allowances in excess of those distributed to covered entities. These allowances are released only if the allowance market price breaches a predetermined price ceiling. Releasing the allowances increases allowance supply and so brings the price back down below the ceiling.

---

[4]   The World Carbon Pricing Database provides a harmonized record of sector coverage and prices in carbon pricing mechanisms implemented worldwide from 1990 to 2020. https://www.rff.org/publications/data-tools/world-carbon-pricing-database/.

[5]   S. Quemin and M. Pahle. 2022. Financials Threaten to Undermine the Functioning of Emissions Markets. *Nature Climate Change*. https://doi.org/10.1038/s41558-022-01560-w.

Box 12

Case Study: Limiting Market Swings in the Regional Greenhouse Gas Initiative

To manage supply and demand and regulate its carbon market, the Regional Greenhouse Gas Initiative implemented two strategic reserves: the Cost Containment Reserve and the Emissions Containment Reserve. The Cost Containment Reserve is approximately 10% of the budget for each participating state. The trigger price—at which the reserve is released—was set at $13.91 in 2022 and will increase by 7% each year. The Emissions Containment Reserve was implemented in 2021. In 2022, the trigger price was set at $6.42 and will increase by 7% per year as well.

Source: Regional Greenhouse Gas Initiative.
https://www.rggi.org/program-overview-and-design/elements.

A cost containment reserve is triggered if prices fall below a predetermined floor, withdrawing allowances from circulation and placing them in the reserve. They can be released when the carbon price rises above the floor (Box 13).

Box 13

Case Study: Market Regulation Tools in the People's Republic of China

The emission trading system of the People's Republic of China employs a cost containment reserve and a buy-back system for allowances in some provinces. The option to return credits to the system's regulatory body reduces the risk of price fluctuation from supply and demand. The use of this system requires a convincing benefit for returning credits to the regulatory body over selling them to participants who are over their allowances.

Source: Asian Development Bank. 2016. *Emissions Trading Schemes and Their Linking: Challenges and Opportunities in Asia and the Pacific.* Manila.
https://www.adb.org/sites/default/files/publication/182501/emissions-trading-schemes.pdf.

An ETS interacts closely with the larger economy and can employ tools used in other markets such as options, futures, forward contracts, and swaps (Box 14). For this market to be well regulated, rules for such vehicles should be promulgated. Policymakers should take the following actions when setting the market structure and should revisit their decisions regularly (PMR and ICAP 2021):

(i)   Establish the rationale for market intervention and recognize associated risks.

(ii)   Establish rules for banking and borrowing. Banking allows participants to establish a safety net by acting early to save some of their unused allowances for use in a future compliance period. Borrowing allows participants to use future carbon allowances in the current compliance period.

(iii)   Establish rules for market participation.

(iv)   Identify the role played by a robust secondary market.

(v)   Choose whether to intervene to address low prices, high prices, or both, as well as the appropriate price- or supply-adjustment intervention.

Box 14

Case Study: Flexible Mechanisms in Japan

Japan's emission trading system clearly defines the various flexibility mechanisms and the range of use allowed.

Offsets. Domestic offset credits from within prefectures can be used toward allowances without restriction, but only one-third of a prefecture's emission reductions can be satisfied by credits from facilities outside of them.

Renewable energy certificates. These are issued for certain projects and count as offsets.

Banking and borrowing. The emission trading system allows banking but not borrowing. Banking is also limited between consecutive compliance periods.

Trading. Only carbon credits related to energy are allowed to be traded under the system.

Source: Asian Development Bank. 2016. *Emissions Trading Schemes and Their Linking: Challenges and Opportunities in Asia and the Pacific.* Manila.
https://www.adb.org/sites/default/files/publication/182501/emissions-trading-schemes.pdf.

Knowledge sharing is helpful in building successful policy. With support from Norway, the United States Agency for International Development, and the European Bank for Reconstruction and Development, Kazakhstan was able to develop protocols for the use of offsets within their ETS. Kazakhstan allows the use of flexible mechanisms that not only benefit the ETS but also help make it more politically palatable and publicly accepted. In the 2014–2015 compliance period, Kazakhstan allowed the use of offsets, borrowing, linking, and joint implementation (ADB 2016a).[6]

Supply and demand play important roles in determining the carbon price. However, as supply is controlled by policymakers who set caps and determine how allowances are distributed, policymakers play a role in determining the price. The carbon price should fluctuate predictably, and price-setting mechanisms should be transparent. As with any market, carbon markets are susceptible to shocks, making flexibility important. As the carbon price itself should not be a barrier to entry for smaller participants, market structure should be a key consideration in designing an ETS, with emission thresholds available to reduce compliance costs for small firms.

7. Ensure compliance and oversight.

A regulatory body is needed to ensure that all participants in an ETS are compliant (Box 15). All sectors and market participants covered by an ETS should be identified and subject to regulation. Compliance can be ensured by managing emission reporting through approved methods, monitoring and approving verifiers and plans, establishing rules and methodologies for market and registry operation, managing approval and verification processes, and designing and enforcing penalties (ADB 2016a). Scope should cover all parts of ETS policy and registry.

---

[6]   Joint Implementation was created under the Kyoto Protocol and allows Annex I covered entities to purchase and apply offsets developed within other Annex I countries.

Case Study: Regulatory Bodies in the People's Republic of China

The emission trading system of the People's Republic of China is organized at both the national and provincial levels. Therefore, oversight comes from two different regulatory bodies that coordinate with each other. Nationally, the State Council Carbon Trading Regulatory Authority develops the basic rules and modalities, while in the provinces, carbon trading regulatory bodies implement, manage, and reinforce these rules.

This dual system applies as well to carbon market registries. Provincial authorities have sub-registries that are aggregated nationally at the end of compliance periods. The country's overall performance toward its nationally determined contribution can thus be tracked.

Source: Asian Development Bank. 2016. *Emissions Trading Schemes and Their Linking: Challenges and Opportunities in Asia and the Pacific.* Manila.
https://www.adb.org/sites/default/files/publication/182501/emissions-trading-schemes.pdf.

A system of penalties—financial and social—can ensure compliance and therefore progress. Financial penalties impose fines for noncompliance, which should, of course, be higher than the costs of compliance with the ETS. Social penalties can include public disclosure and criminal sanctions. The regulatory body should determine the best way to enforce rules, modalities, and penalties (Box 16).

The regulatory body also approves and manages third-party verifiers. An external verification process ensures that all reporting is accurate and transparent, reinforcing ETS reliability and trust in it. This also helps to prevent double-counting, leakage, and other concerns over emission inventories.

Case Study: Regulatory Considerations in India

The Gujarat emission trading system is regulated by the existing Gujarat Pollution Control Board. This body determines the rules and modalities for all the processes included under the emission trading system. It approves participants and ensures that all monitoring and reporting is accurate and transparent.

The Gujarat Pollution Control Board is also responsible for enforcing compliance and penalizing participants who do not follow compliance regulations. It established environmental damage compensation of ₹200/kilogram of emissions over the allowance. All participants in this system must submit an environmental damage deposit to participate. This deposit is determined by their baseline assessment.

Source: IndiaSpend. *Explained: How Surat's Emissions Trading Scheme Works to Reduce Air Pollution.*
https://www.indiaspend.com/explainers/surat-emission-trading-scheme-gujarat-works-to-reduce-air-pollution-763554.

8. Consider flexible mechanisms.

Flexible mechanisms can lower the cost of achieving emission targets. Three flexible mechanisms that can help a covered entity meet its allowance requirement are offsets, banking, and borrowing. The mechanisms selected must depend on its benefits specific to the ETS and country. Flexibility allows a higher participation rate by lowering barriers to entry.

Banking and borrowing were introduced above. Their main disadvantage is that they can reduce abatement overall. So can offsets. Offsets offer geographic flexibility, allowing emission reduction or sequestration that occurs outside of the ETS, either internationally or domestically, to compensate for surplus emissions within it. Offsets are typically generated through projects—such as for methane destruction, forest conservation, or energy efficiency—and can provide lower-cost mitigation opportunities outside ETS scope (Greenhouse Gas Management Institute and Stockholm Environment Institute, n.d.). The first example of international carbon offsets developed is the Clean Development Mechanism of the Kyoto Protocol.

Offsets must be carefully designed to avoid abuse, and many ETSs place limits on their use to meet emission caps. As offsets use reductions achieved outside of covered entities, they introduce quality control challenges. To ensure quality, offsets must be real, additional, verifiable, quantifiable, and enforceable. Several organizations, such as Gold Standard and Verra, currently verify and certify offsets. In the future, Article 6.4 of the Paris Agreement will govern the creation of a global carbon market overseen by a supervisory body that will issue credits, termed A6.4ERs. This will better standardize assurance of the quality and certification of offsets (Dufrasne 2021; Carbon Market Institute, n.d.).

An ETS must specify the protocols under which offsets are generated, and offsets should be verified by third parties. If offsets are purchased from entities in other countries, the rules of the Paris Agreement are important. Article 6 limits the use of offsets in meeting caps and mitigation goals because they can reduce direct mitigation achieved by the ETS itself.

9. Consider linking.

Linking ETSs permits emission allowances from one ETS to be used in another. Linking creates a larger carbon market, which adds liquidity and increases price competition. Covered entities may be able to access allowances priced lower than those within their own ETS, thereby reducing the overall cost of emission reduction and generating economic efficiencies. As ETSs become linked, their carbon prices converge, which can mitigate concerns over economic competitiveness and reduce the risk of leakage (Partnership for Market Readiness and ICAP 2021). Knowledge sharing and international cooperation can also reduce duplication of efforts in research and development. Further, eventual participation in linkages can make emission trading policy more politically palatable. While linking can offer many benefits to individual countries, it poses some risks and requires flexibility in ETS design to ensure alignment in a joint market (Table 1).

Table 1: Benefits and Risks of Linkage

	Benefits	Risks
Economic	+ Lowers aggregate compliance costs across systems + Increases market liquidity and depth + Can reduce leakage and competitiveness concerns + Can attract external resources for reducing emissions	– Can increase domestic emissions and reduce environmental and social co-benefits
	± Can promote price stability, though it can also import price volatility from abroad ± Can prompt significant financial transfers ± May create administrative efficiencies: pre-linkage negotiations and possible program modifications can be costly, while linked systems may lower administrative costs through pooled resources	
Political	+ May strengthen domestic emission trading system legitimacy and durability through reduced costs and international collaboration + May increase potential for raising ambition	– May create domestic political concerns over distributional impacts and resource transfers abroad
	± Can help shape and build momentum on global climate action, but also decreases independent control over program design and ambition	
Environmental	+ Can encourage policymakers to adopt a more ambitious target given the cost-efficiency gains from linking	– Linking to a system that is not equally robust can incentivize weak reduction targets

Source: Emissions Trading Worldwide – International Carbon Action Partnership Status Report 2022, Table 9.2, p. 198. https://icapcarbonaction.com/system/files/document/ets-handbook-2020_finalweb.pdf.

Examples of linked systems include the EU with Switzerland, subnational systems in the PRC; Tokyo and Saitama in Japan; California and Québec; and the RGGI system in northeastern US states (Figure 5 and Box 17). While linking is usually done after establishing an ETS, the RGGI system was planned for linkage from the start. It may be wise to consider linkage opportunities during development to ensure benefits globally and in each individual country. More complex linkage structures are possible, including using offset credits generated by a crediting system like the Clean Development Mechanism or one-way linkages.

Box 17

Case Study: Linkage in the Regional Greenhouse Gas Initiative

The Regional Greenhouse Gas Initiative (RGGI) is a linkage arrangement among several states in the northeast and mid-Atlantic United States that operates an independent emission trading system (ETS) covering their electric power sector. Each state develops its ETS policy and issues allowances within the framework set by a common operating body. The RGGI sets a cap for each compliance period based on the region's emissions from the power sector, and allowances are distributed through an auction and must be surrendered at the end of the 3-year compliance period according to emission levels. Trading is allowed among all states in the ETS. This linkage system has proved successful in reducing greenhouse gas emissions, decoupling emissions from economic growth, and increasing net economic benefits.

Source: Asian Development Bank. 2016. *Emissions Trading Schemes and Their Linking: Challenges and Opportunities in Asia and the Pacific*. Manila. https://www.adb.org/sites/default/files/publication/182501/emissions-trading-schemes.pdf.

Figure 5: Linked Emission Trading Systems

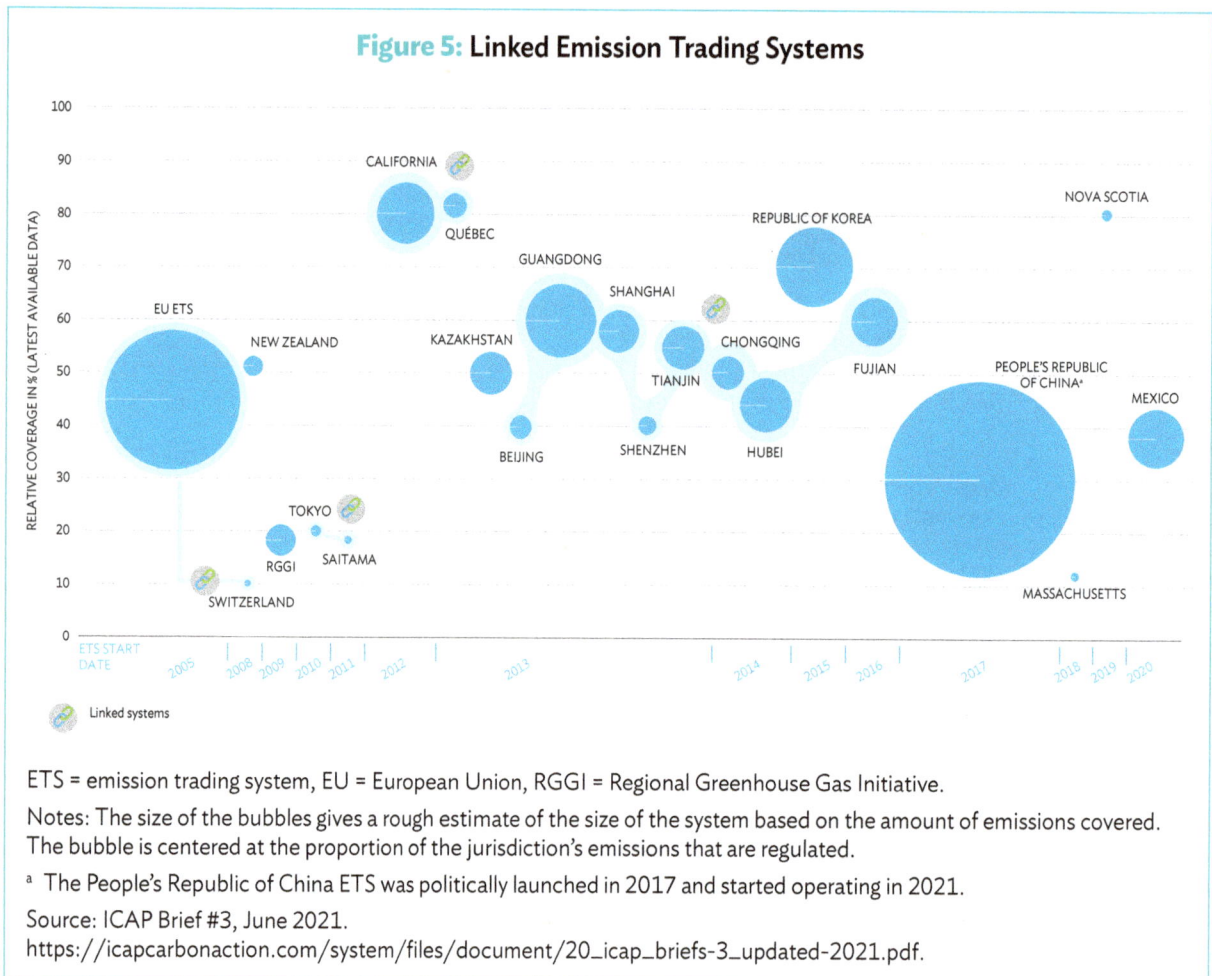

ETS = emission trading system, EU = European Union, RGGI = Regional Greenhouse Gas Initiative.

Notes: The size of the bubbles gives a rough estimate of the size of the system based on the amount of emissions covered. The bubble is centered at the proportion of the jurisdiction's emissions that are regulated.

a The People's Republic of China ETS was politically launched in 2017 and started operating in 2021.

Source: ICAP Brief #3, June 2021.
https://icapcarbonaction.com/system/files/document/20_icap_briefs-3_updated-2021.pdf.

10. Implement, evaluate, and improve.

At the start of operations, two options are available to the implementing authority: pilots and phasing in. Pilot programs usually involve a small segment of the entities that will ultimately be regulated. They may be defined geographically, as in the PRC. Phased-in programs may be defined in terms of the total emissions an entity produces. The advantage of including only large emitters in the first phase is that they are more likely to have the resources needed for implementation. The implementing authority may also choose to phase in requirements for monitoring, reporting, and verification.

Policy evaluation metrics are recommended to promote regular progress through ETS development. These metrics allow internal evaluation in addition to external checking and review of compliance. Ongoing research and development are encouraged as the development of ETSs across the globe is still in its infancy.

Evaluation should cover the monitoring, reporting, and verification phases of an ETS. Policymakers should decide on the timing, process, and scope for reviews. Greater specificity ensures the evaluations will identify flaws and needed changes in ETS policy design. Evaluations should engage all stakeholders to ensure that the system is operating as intended across sectors and departments (Box 18).

Box 18

Case Study: Evaluating and Improving in Kazakhstan

Despite the promised benefits of an emission trading system (ETS), it is not always guaranteed to work. Kazakhstan's ETS saw negative impacts. Carbon dioxide emissions and the intensity of the power sector there grew rather than decreased. Policy reevaluation is therefore necessary to address any unforeseen circumstances or errors in the policy.

An analysis commissioned by Kazakhstan demonstrated ways to effectively redesign its ETS by increasing stakeholder engagement and addressing deficiencies in carbon allocation and trading.

Source: Environmental Defense Fund. 2016. *Kazakhstan: An Emissions Trading Case Study*.
https://www.ieta.org/resources/Resources/Case_Studies_Worlds_Carbon_Markets/2016/Kazakhstan_Case_Study_2016.pdf.

Stakeholders can help identify flaws and options for improvements using a cross-disciplinary lens. Opportunities for linking to another ETS should be revisited during regular program evaluations.

D. Mitigating Potential Challenges

A well-designed ETS combined with strong monitoring and evaluation systems can propel a country toward its emission reduction goals. However, like any policy tool, an ETS can pose a wide range of challenges. The following section presents some of the more common challenges and suggests mitigation strategies.

1. Maintaining economic competitiveness

One common concern when introducing an ETS is its potential effect on the economy. Concerns can center on economic competitiveness relative to other countries, as well as on impacts on specific regulated sectors.

Maintaining economic competitiveness with other countries is tied to the question of leakage. Leakage is the movement of carbon emissions from one jurisdiction with more stringent emission policies to another with less stringent policies. The two main types of leakage are production leakage and capital leakage. Production leakage occurs when a firm shifts some production to less-regulated jurisdictions in response to increased operating cost under an ETS. Capital leakage occurs when a firm reduces its investment in anticipation of lower profitability under an ETS. Because it affects long-term economic investments, capital leakage can be more damaging and have more permanent effects. Beyond economics, leakage can have negative political ramifications. Further, it undermines ETS objectives as emissions are shifted geographically rather than reduced.

While leakage is a serious concern when designing and implementing an ETS, little evidence of it exists in practice. In most jurisdictions, carbon prices are not yet high enough to substantially affect the economics of production, and free allowances are sometimes used to prevent any potential leakage. Moreover, with growing focus on emission reduction globally, and with most countries enacting policies to reach their NDC objectives, few countries will remain in which firms can escape emission regulations.

Further, the EU and others are considering the introduction of carbon border adjustment mechanisms to prevent leakage by applying a fee to imported goods to account for differentials in emissions generated in their production (Center for Climate and Energy Solutions, n.d.).

To mitigate potential negative impacts on regulated sectors, governments can adopt free allocation, use auction proceeds to cushion covered entities from economic impacts, or provide them other financial assistance or tax relief. A government that adopts any of these strategies must balance economic competitiveness with incentives to reduce emissions. Governments may phase out free allocation or other assistance over time, thereby softening negative economic impacts in the early days of ETS implementation while still moving later toward its emission reduction goals. This is one example of how creating an ETS requires long-term strategic thinking.

2. Voluntary markets

Voluntary carbon markets enable companies to purchase carbon credits or offsets to meet internal climate goals. Voluntary markets have grown substantially in recent years, reaching $1 billion in November 2021, and new guidelines for international cooperation under Article 6 may increase demand in the future. The spread of corporate net-zero commitments in the private sector is likely to drive further rapid growth in voluntary carbon markets in the coming years (World Bank 2022).

While voluntary markets can offer lower-cost alternatives for covered entities to meet their emission cap, extensive use of international carbon offset credits can disrupt an ETS market. Specifically, the introduction of carbon offsets can generate an allowance surplus and force down prices while undermining incentives for covered entities to reduce domestic emissions. If the price of international offset credits falls below domestic carbon prices, the upshot could be no actual emission reductions within the country. Because of this risk, many ETSs either limit the use of international offsets or prohibit them altogether. If an ETS allows offsets, parameters for their incorporation must be strategically designed to prevent overreliance on international offsets to meet domestic caps.

3. Fraud and market manipulation

Several characteristics of ETSs make them susceptible to fraud and market manipulation: the lack of a physical commodity, large amounts of money involved, and a wide range of individual systems and derivative markets with immature regulations and little oversight and transparency. Types of fraud can include overreporting emission reductions; selling allowances that do not exist or belong to the seller; and exploiting weak regulations to commit money laundering, securities or tax fraud, or other financial crimes. State-owned enterprises enable a distinct form of market manipulation. State energy monopolies and the challenges posed by dysfunctional, loss-making state-owned enterprises in energy may block effective ETS design.

As participants must trust an ETS for it to function effectively and efficiently, a strong focus on transparency and oversight is essential from the outset of planning. The risk of fraud can be addressed by establishing a strong legal framework to regulate the market, independent verification, and robust enforcement mechanisms, thereby maintaining confidence in the system (Interpol Environmental Crimes Programme 2013).

E. Resources to Support Emission Trading System Development and Implementation

DMCs looking for support in developing an ETS, as part of their efforts to reduce GHG emissions and address commitments under the Paris Agreement, will find assistance in all facets of capacity development, planning, and implementation.

ADB's regional departments provide support through country programming. Under its Carbon Market 2.0 Program, ADB operates the following programs that can support DMC adoption and rollout of ETSs (Figure 6):

(i)   The Technical Support Facility helps a DMC exploit Clean Development Mechanism projects.

(ii)   The Article 6 Support Facility helps countries establish and participate in domestic, bilateral, and international carbon markets consistent with conditional NDCs.

(iii) The Climate Action Catalyst Fund provides carbon finance to DMCs through internationally transferred mitigation outcomes.

(iv)   The Credit Marketing Facility offers knowledge resources that DMCs can use to design offset contracts and maximize financial returns on offset projects.

(v)   The Japan Fund for the Joint Crediting Mechanism provides grants and technical assistance via an internationally transferred mitigation outcomes partnership between a DMC and Japan.

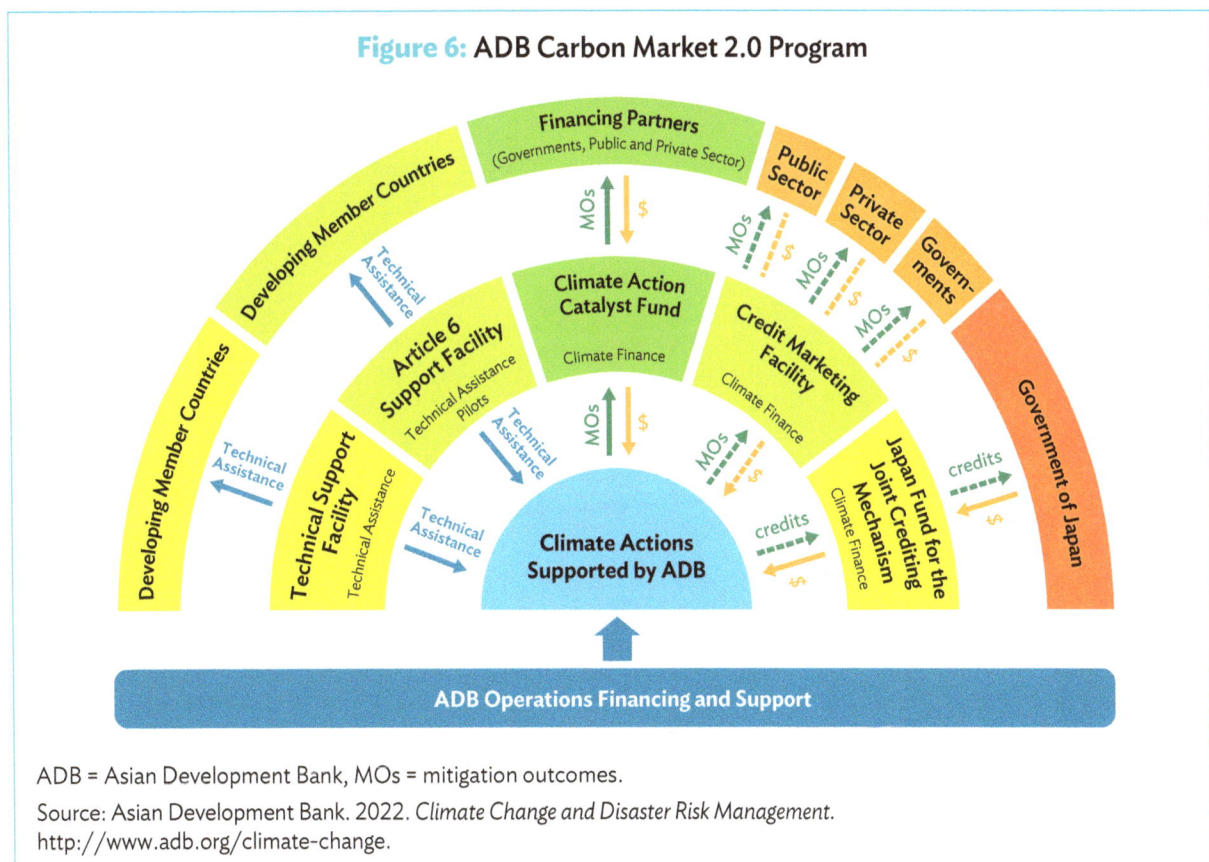

Figure 6: ADB Carbon Market 2.0 Program

ADB = Asian Development Bank, MOs = mitigation outcomes.
Source: Asian Development Bank. 2022. *Climate Change and Disaster Risk Management.* http://www.adb.org/climate-change.

Other networks that provide resources and technical guidance and facilitate cross-country collaboration on ETSs include the following:

(i)   The Partnership for Market Implementation helps countries design, pilot, and implement carbon pricing instruments and benefit from Article 6 of the Paris Agreement. Bangladesh, India, Indonesia, Kazakhstan, Malaysia, Pakistan, the PRC, Thailand, and Viet Nam are currently participating.

(ii)   The International Carbon Action Partnership (ICAP) provides a forum for cooperation and learning among members to facilitate links between ETSs with the goal of creating a well-functioning global carbon market. Kazakhstan participates in ICAP as an observer.

(iii)   The Carbon Pricing Leadership Coalition facilitates partnerships on subjects like internal carbon pricing in businesses, and research and communication on carbon pricing. India, Kazakhstan, and Pakistan now participate.

3 CARBON TAXATION

A. Introduction

Many ADB developing member countries (DMCs) levy excises on motor fuels and other energy products that implicitly price carbon. Recently receiving considerable attention is the opportunity countries have to complement such taxes with explicit carbon pricing or to transform excises into a more consistent carbon pricing framework aligned with different fuels' carbon emissions (Figure 7), toward meeting their nationally determined contributions (NDCs) to climate change mitigation (Box 19).

Figure 7: Carbon Pricing and Excises on Energy

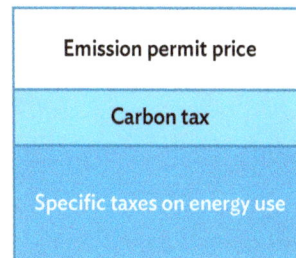

Note: Carbon pricing can be explicit through carbon taxation and emission trading or implicit via specific taxes on energy use.
Source: Organisation for Economic Co-operation and Development (2018).

Box 19

Snapshot of Cumulative Emissions

Carbon dioxide (CO_2) emissions have increased rapidly over the past 2 decades, effectively doubling in most of the larger Asian countries and increasing the region's historical cumulative CO_2 emissions (box figure).[a] In terms of contemporary CO_2 emissions per capita, some developing member countries now exceed the European Union, notably Malaysia, Mongolia, and the People's Republic of China. Kazakhstan, Palau, and Turkmenistan compare with the United States, and more economies are on a trajectory to do so.[b] Small island states and others with modest emissions per capita may strengthen their demands for carbon taxes on the maritime sector and by higher-income countries by practicing it themselves.[c]

Cumulative Emissions of World Regions

PRC = People's Republic of China.

[a] M. Crippa et al. 2021. *Fossil CO₂ Emissions of All World Countries*. Ispra, Italy: Joint Research Centre. https://publications.jrc.ec.europa.eu/repository/handle/JRC121460.

[b] Australia, Brunei Darussalam, Japan, New Zealand, the Republic of Korea, Singapore, and Taipei,China also exceed European Union CO_2 emissions per capita.

[c] Radio New Zealand. 2021. *Marshall and Solomons Urge Carbon Tax for Shipping Industry*. 16 March. https://www.rnz.co.nz/international/pacific-news/438514/marshall-and-solomons-urge-carbon-tax-for-shipping-industry.

Source: Our World in Data, the Global Carbon Project.

1. The Asia and Pacific context for carbon taxes

While carbon taxes have for long been used in several member countries in the Organisation for Economic Co-operation and Development (OECD)—Canada, France, Ireland, Japan, Portugal, Switzerland, the United Kingdom, the five Nordic countries, and others—a range of emerging economies have more recently implemented carbon taxation, following the Paris Agreement: Argentina, Chile, Colombia, Mexico, Singapore, South Africa, and Ukraine. Among ADB DMCs, Indonesia recently passed legislation to tax carbon (Cekindo 2022), and others analyzing the option include the Philippines (Villanueva 2021), Thailand (Chantanusornsiri 2021), and Malaysia (Yong 2021). Meanwhile, the People's Republic of China (PRC), Kazakhstan, and Viet Nam have already implemented emissions trading with carbon allowances.

Carbon taxation is more straightforward administratively than carbon pricing with an emission trading system (ETS), especially if a country already levies excises on energy products. Taxing the carbon content of fuel requires control over a limited number of importers and producers of energy products. While an ETS often requires many allowances to be handed out for free, carbon taxation brings in revenue that can be used to alleviate the associated challenges. The revenue collected can help finance the transformation of energy and transport systems and land use practices that produce greenhouse gases (GHGs) while channeling support to low-income groups and biodiversity protection. A frequently applied revenue recycling mechanism is to lower taxes that distort employment and inhibit economic growth, such as payroll and income taxes. In practice, governments with carbon taxes have opted for a mixture of revenue uses attuned to national circumstances and priorities.

Integrating a carbon tax into a wider macroeconomic package of fiscal measures to underpin economic development is often the best way to balance various interests, compensate vulnerable groups, minimize opposition, and obtain positive macroeconomic impacts overall.

The current peak in world market energy prices caused by the Russian invasion of Ukraine could provide an opportunity to implement carbon taxation once prices begin to normalize, provided that governments have the fiscal and legislative framework ready.

2. Objectives of carbon taxation

Mitigation pledges. Carbon taxation can help close the gap between business-as-usual trends in GHG emissions and the reduction targets pledged by countries in their NDCs under the United Nations Framework Convention on Climate Change (UNFCCC) and the Paris Agreement. At the 26th Conference of the Parties, the Glasgow Climate Pact called on countries to revisit and strengthen targets in their NDCs, providing an occasion to explore in detail how carbon taxation could be applied. Current NDCs are not sufficiently ambitious to effectuate the reductions required by 2030 to hold global temperature increase to 2°C.

Experience in several countries shows that carbon taxation curbs emissions, confirming what numerous economic simulations suggest. A recent econometric study of the carbon tax in France has shown how gradually increasing the carbon tax rate caused emissions to decline while simultaneously increasing employment in small and medium-sized low-carbon businesses (Dussaux 2019).

While some large and carbon-intensive industries responded to the carbon tax by curbing their output, the tax did not damage national economic growth or employment overall. Ex-post studies of carbon taxes in other European countries and Canada have reported comparable findings (Andersen and Ekins 2009, Rivers and Schaufele 2015). Moreover, carbon taxation offers a less costly pathway toward mitigation than policy instruments that rely on command and control, tax expenditure, or direct subsidies.

The contribution of a carbon tax to mitigation depends on the sectors covered and the tax rate applied. The tax rate needed to close the gap of an NDC will differ by country because emitters' price responsiveness differs according to the fuels and technologies in use. An analysis by the International Monetary Fund (IMF) showed that a tax rate of $25 per ton of CO_2 would suffice to accomplish the PRC's NDC target, but the Republic of Korea requires a tax rate of $75 to meet its NDC, in part because its pledge is more stringent (IMF and OECD 2021).

However, all carbon taxes begin low and rise incrementally to give polluters time to adjust. Analogous with gradual global warming, a gradually increasing carbon tax will alter and transform the economics of energy use over time.

Fiscal policies and energy security. A significant macroeconomic feature of carbon pricing is relief for the balance of payments with lower fuel imports and a demand shift toward domestic supply. Moreover, many countries will strengthen their energy security as low-carbon energy sources like solar, wind, and geothermal replace imported fossil fuel.

Synergy with emissions trading. Carbon taxation and ETSs are equally efficient approaches to carbon pricing, at least in theory. While ETSs cap total emissions but allow the carbon price to fluctuate, a carbon tax provides a fixed price but leaves a bit uncertain the exact implications for emissions. However, individual households and other small emitters cannot easily be subject to an ETS and are obvious candidates for a complementary carbon tax. Several European Union (EU) countries have domestic carbon taxes for sectors not covered by its ETS, aiming to set the carbon tax rate to reflect the carbon price in the ETS. Parity between the carbon allowance price and the carbon tax sends a consistent price signal to decarbonize across the economy. Moreover, a floor price for the carbon market, as practiced in the United Kingdom, can counteract frequent volatility in carbon markets. The floor price kicks in as a surplus carbon tax when the price of emissions allowances declines below a predefined threshold. This maintains a minimum price on carbon, which provides security to investors in low-carbon transformation.

B. Step-by-Step Guide to Introduce Carbon Taxation

1. Identify the mitigation gap and priority sectors.

Based on an update of a country's NDC, the overall gap to targets is identified, as is which sectors contribute most significantly to national emissions. Further, projections can show which sectors are likely to increase their emissions under business as usual, or a scenario without government action. Ever-increasing demand for transportation has spurred high growth in demand for motor fuels, frequently making transportation the sector most critical to excessive emissions.

Other sectors that are strong candidates for a carbon tax are electric power generation, industry, and household heating and cooling. In all of them, cleaner technologies are available to substitute for fossil fuels, but they struggle to compete in the market if fossil fuels are not held accountable for their external costs from global warming and air pollution. The NDC could be extended with estimations of the relative costs of curbing emissions in various sectors, which would be useful information for modeling the economic impacts of carbon pricing (Figure 8).

Figure 8: The 100-Year Global Warming Potential of Greenhouse Gases

Greenhouse Gas	Formula	100-Year GWP
Carbon dioxide	CO_2	1
Methane	CH_4	25
Nitrous oxide	N_2O	298
Sulfur hexafluoride	SF_6	22,800
Hydrofluorocarbon-23	CHF_3	14,800
Hydrofluorocarbon-32	CH_2F_2	675
Perfluoromethane	CF_4	7,390
Perfluoroethane	C_2F_6	12,200
Perfluoropropane	C_3F_8	8,830
Perfluorobutane	C_4F_{10}	8,860
Perfluorocyclobutane	$c\text{-}C_4F_8$	10,300
Perfluoropentane	C_5F_{12}	13,300
Perfluorohexane	C_6F_{14}	9,300

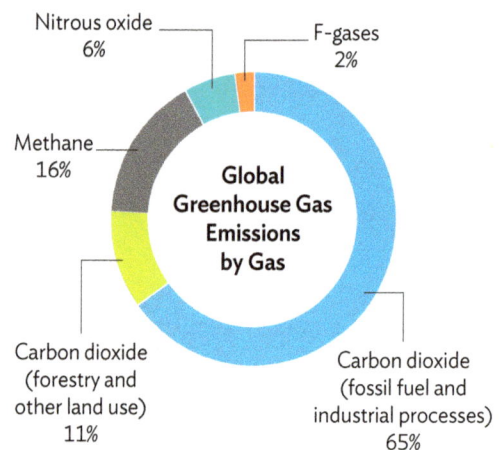

GWP = global warming potential.

Note: The pie chart shows shares of global emissions in carbon dioxide equivalent.

Source: United Nations Framework Convention on Climate Change.

---

2. Identify greenhouse gases to be taxed.

There are GHGs other than CO_2, notably methane from landfills used in waste management and from livestock, and nitrous oxides from fertilizers used in agriculture and forestry. The industrial F-gases hydrofluorocarbons, perfluorocarbons, and sulfur hexafluoride have large global warming potential and, despite their few users, have climate change CO_2-equivalent consequences that make them relevant to carbon pricing, as seen in some countries. Global warming potential multipliers (shown in Figure 9) can be used to determine a tax rate for GHG emissions other than CO_2 that reflect their CO_2 equivalence.

With a so-called fuel approach to taxing CO_2 and its equivalents, all importers and producers of fossil fuels and biofuels must be required to register with the national tax authority (UN 2001). The same requirement applies to importers and producers of industrial F-gases. The carbon tax law must obligate all these entities to report to the tax authority monthly or quarterly the quantities of fuels or F-gases imported or produced and sold. The resulting emissions can then be determined based on the emissions coefficients of UNFCCC accounting methodology, reducing the need for costly monitoring equipment (UN Climate Change[b], n.d.). However, for some emitters, a direct emissions approach will be needed as tax base (Tables 2 and 3). For instance, nonfuel emissions from certain industrial processes (for example, mineralogical) are often substantial and need to be reported by individual firms.

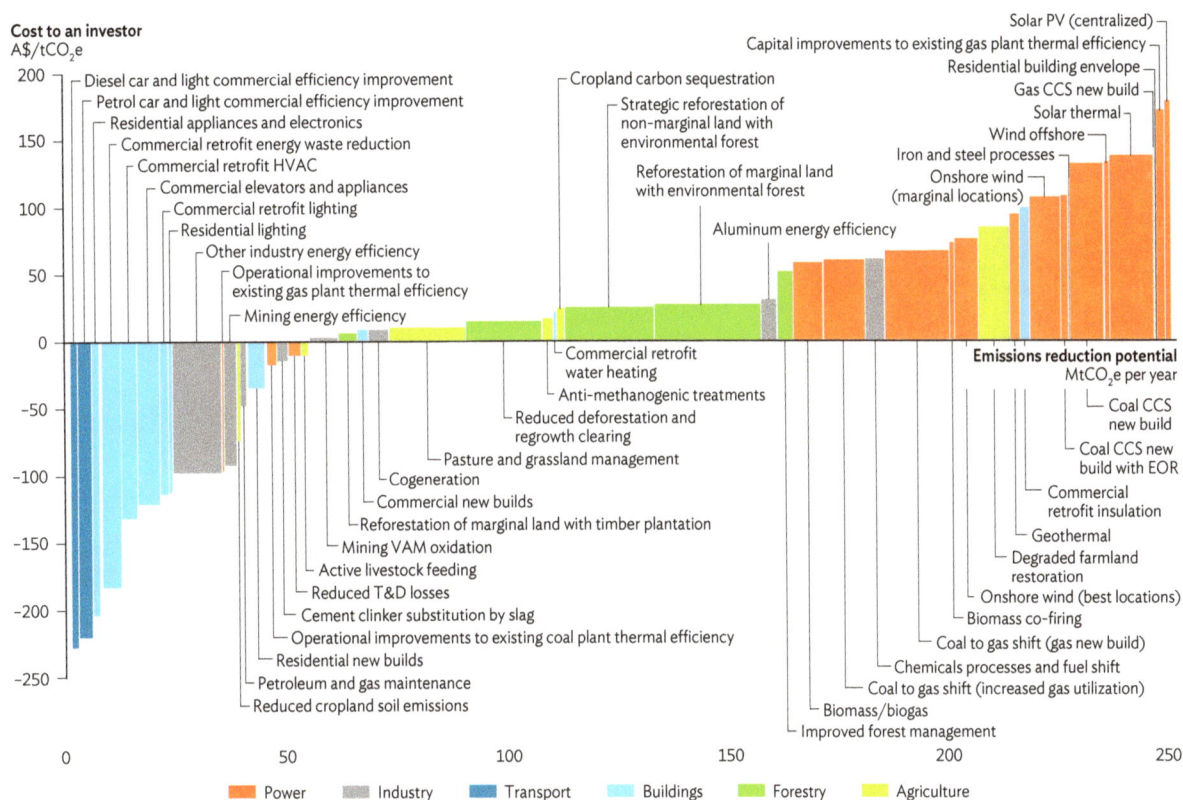

Figure 9: Marginal Cost Curve for Mitigation Options in Australia

CCS = carbon capture and storage; EOR = enhanced oil recovery; HVAC = heating, ventilation, and air conditioning; $MtCO_2e$ = metric tons of carbon dioxide equivalent; Mtpa = metric tons per annum; PV = photovoltaic; T&D = transmission and distribution; VAM = ventilation air methane.

Notes: Lowest-cost opportunities to reduce emissions by 249 tons of carbon dioxide equivalent—includes only opportunities required to reach emission reduction target of 249 Mtpa (25% reduction on 2000 emissions); excludes opportunities involving a significant lifestyle element or consumption decision, changes in business/activity mix, and opportunities with a high degree of speculation or technological uncertainty.

Source: ClimateWorks Foundation.

Table 2: Fuel Approach to Tax Carbon Emissions

1. Tax base	→	Fuels
2. Tax rate	→	Applied to different fuels
3. Taxable event/point of regulation	→	Anywhere in the value chain
4. Administration	→	Typically, existing excise tax administration
5. Coverage	→	Usually, main fuel sources
6. How to calculate tax rate	→	Depends on carbon content, some jurisdictions use carbon content and others the value chain
7. How tax rates are presented	→	By volume or weight units
8. Calculating total tax liability	→	Based on total fuel use/combusted
9. Special considerations	→	Different fuel qualities and biofuel mixtures

Source: United Nations. 2001. United Nations Handbook on Carbon Taxation for Developing Countries.
https://www.un.org/development/desa/financing/document/un-handbook-carbon-taxation-developing-countries-2021.

Table 3: Direct Emissions Approach to Tax Carbon Emissions

1. Tax base	→	Emissions
2. Tax rate	→	Applied to emissions
3. Taxable event/point of regulation	→	At the emission source, definition of facility requried
4. Administration	→	Require new MRV administration
5. Coverage	→	Usually, large facilities
6. How to calculate tax rate	→	No correction is required
7. Calculating total tax liability	→	Based on total emissions
8. Special considerations	→	MRV system required

MRV = monitoring, reporting, verification.
Source: United Nations. 2001. United Nations Handbook on Carbon Taxation for Developing Countries.
https://www.un.org/development/desa/financing/document/un-handbook-carbon-taxation-developing-countries-2021.

3. Assess implications for specific fuels and risks of carbon leakage.

With the fuel approach to carbon taxation, coal and heavy fuel oils become more expensive because of their high carbon content, while gasoline, diesel, and natural gas are less affected. With the direct emissions approach, industries using coal and heavy fuel oils are most affected (Box 20). In relation to biofuels, carbon content can be established with a life-cycle assessment (Bird et al. 2013). It may be administratively challenging to capture all domestic streams of biomass sourced for energy generation, but the main emitters should be included. The carbon tax on electricity generation can be imposed either on the fuels used or on their emissions, delivering a competitive advantage to low-carbon renewables such as solar and wind. A tax on electricity end users per kilowatt-hour consumed would not differentiate appropriately.

When importers and producers pass on carbon tax costs to customers in product prices, market prices change in favor of low-carbon technologies. However, risks emerge of carbon leakage from energy-intensive industries open to trade. Carbon leakage is when producers in countries with a carbon price lose market share to producers in countries without one. Six key industries raise concerns: iron and steel, aluminum, cement and lime, pulp and paper, basic chemicals, and petroleum refining. In countries with developed industrial bases, these six industries may easily account for half of all industrial emissions despite their contribution to gross domestic product being only a few percent. Exempting them fully from carbon tax would thus shift a huge reduction burden onto other sectors. Ways therefore need to be found to integrate these emitters wisely in the scheme (see step 6 below). These sectors are not equally tradable because of differences in product ratios of value to weight, with cement, for example, far less tradable than iron and steel. Fishing fleets are also at risk because of their high share of fuel costs in turnover.

Box 20

Emission Factors

Excise taxes on energy products are typically based on weight or volume, but a carbon tax needs to be based on carbon dioxide (CO_2) emissions. Handy tables with CO_2 emission factors for most fossil fuels and biofuels are available in Annex VI to the Commission Implementing Regulation (EU) 2018/2066 on the monitoring and reporting of greenhouse gas emissions (box table).[a] This source also provides CO_2 equivalence factors for other types of emissions, such as from mineralogical processes. All emission factors are based on guidance from the Intergovernmental Panel on Climate Change.

Table: **Fuel Emission Factors against Net Calorific Value**

Fuel Type Description	Emission Factor (tCO_2/TJ)	Net Calorific Value (TJ/Gg)	Source
Crude oil	73.3	42.3	IPCC 2006 GL
Orimulsion	77.0	27.5	IPCC 2006 GL
Natural gas liquids	64.2	44.2	IPCC 2006 GL
Motor gasoline	69.3	44.3	IPCC 2006 GL
Kerosene (other than jet kerosene)	71.9	43.8	IPCC 2006 GL
Shale oil	73.3	38.1	IPCC 2006 GL
Gas/diesel oil	74.1	43.0	IPCC 2006 GL
Residual fuel oil	77.4	40.4	IPCC 2006 GL
Liquefied petroleum gases	63.1	47.3	IPCC 2006 GL

GL = guidelines, IPCC = Intergovernmental Panel on Climate Change, tCO_2/TJ = tons of carbon dioxide per terajoule, TJ/Gg = terajoules per gigagram.

[a] EUR-Lex. *Commission Implementing Regulation (EU) 2018/2066 of 19 December 2018 on the Monitoring and Reporting of Greenhouse Gas Emissions Pursuant to Directive 2003/87/EC of the European Parliament and of the Council and Amending Commission Regulation (EU) No. 601/2012 (Text with EEA Relevance).* https://eur-lex.europa.eu/legal-content/en/TXT/?uri=CELEX%3A32018R2066.

Source: European Commission.

4. Assess distributional impacts.

The implication of carbon taxation for low-income groups is an important challenge. Poor households often cannot afford to upgrade their homes, domestic appliances, or vehicles for better fuel efficiency. It has nevertheless been shown that, in most middle-income countries, carbon pricing has progressive effects, penalizing higher-income households more because energy use and vehicle ownership tend to increase with income (Dorband et al. 2019). One caveat, however, pertains to different patterns of energy expenditure between urban and rural households (Koh et al. 2021). Urban households have higher costs for transportation and less opportunity to use biomass for fuel than rural households. Studies that have explored this divide find that the urban poor people in developing countries will suffer under carbon pricing unless revenue recycling mechanisms compensate them. Considering the modest income of the lowest deciles and impacts in the range of a few percent, it is financially feasible to offset their burdens with targeted assistance. Still, it may be difficult to reach low-income households, especially those living below the poverty line. Possible strategies to mitigate impacts on low-income households are further discussed below.

5. Calibrate the carbon tax rate.

The carbon tax rate should, in principle, be uniform per unit of carbon emitted across different energy products and sectors, if not from its inception then soon after. Incrementally raising the tax from an initially modest rate can give polluters time to adjust, help overcome political resistance, and enable learning on mitigation options. To avoid revenue erosion, it is essential that legislation on the carbon tax mandates automatic annual tax rate adjustments based on the consumer price index. The IMF considers it appropriate to aim for a rate of $25 per ton of carbon dioxide equivalent for low-income emerging economies, $50 for middle-income emerging economies, and $75 for advanced economies by 2030 to meet the Paris Agreement's target of limiting global warming below 2°C (Parry, Black, and Roaf 2021). Because purchasing power and labor costs differ in emerging economies, the carbon tax rate will not need to reach rates seen in some OECD countries. Integrated energy sector and economic modeling can help determine what carbon tax rate will be required to close a country's NDC emission gap (Box 21). Such models need to make assumptions about behavioral responses. Rather than rely on stylized general equilibrium models with little disaggregated data, it is better to use or develop econometric energy sector models based on time series data (e.g., as in Soocheol, Pollitt, and Ueta 2012).

Box 21

Using Carbon Tax to Close Mitigation Gaps in Denmark

Green tax reform in Denmark in 2022 aims to increase the carbon tax rate gradually to €100 per ton of carbon dioxide by 2030. There will be a complementary carbon price floor for emitters in the emissions trading system. The carbon tax increase will close a mitigation gap in the business sector, allowing Denmark to meet its target of a 70% reduction relative to 1990 by 2030, provided that agriculture also delivers on its reduction target.

Trend in Denmark's Carbon Dioxide Emissions from Energy Use

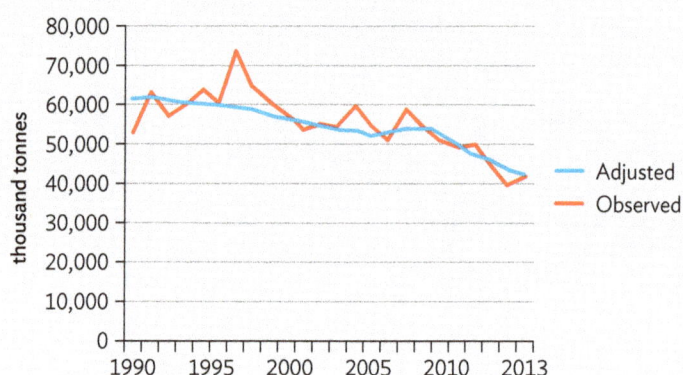

Source: Danish Energy Agency. https://ens.dk/en/press/danish-carbon-emissions-continue-drop; and https://www.cepweb.org/denmarks-green-tax-reform-g20-countries-should-take-notice/.

---

6. Determine scope for reductions or exemptions.

Market prices for energy products vary considerably, and they are traded at prices rather removed from their energy and carbon content. A uniform carbon tax would have more impact on the price of coal than on other energy sources (Table 4). This has implications for businesses that depend heavily on coal, such as cement and steel makers. To avoid complete exemptions, different methods can be used to maintain incentives in a carbon tax scheme. Some Latin American countries allow major emitters to use carbon offsets acquired in voluntary carbon markets to meet part of their tax liability.

Table 4: Illustrative Energy Price Impacts for a Carbon Tax of $50 per Ton of Carbon Dioxide by 2030

Country	Coal Baseline Price, $/GJ	Coal Price Increase (%)	Natural Gas Baseline Price, $/GJ	Natural Gas Price Increase (%)	Electricity Baseline Price, $/kWh	Electricity Price Increase (%)	Gasoline Baseline Price, $/liter	Gasoline Price Increase (%)
Argentina	2.9	172	3.7	86	0.08	18	1.14	13
Australia	3.4	154	7.9	37	0.12	25	1.13	12
Brazil	4.4	122	9.2	34	0.07	7	1.23	8
Canada	2.6	209	4.2	69	0.08	10	1.14	11
PRC	4.4	114	10.5	25	0.05	46	1.13	12
France	6.2	94	15.8	18	0.13	2	1.77	9
Germany	5.8	91	12.4	23	0.17	9	1.74	8
India	5.0	99	3.5	98	0.06	47	1.12	12
Indonesia	2.7	187	5.7	44	0.08	57	0.45	31
Italy	4.6	116	15.4	24	0.12	11	1.90	8
Japan	3.7	132	11.1	24	0.12	24	1.37	10
Mexico	1.8	284	3.0	91	0.09	26	0.97	14
Russian Federation	2.2	209	2.7	95	0.08	36	0.73	18
Saudi Arabia			3.9	69	0.10	33	0.27	45
South Africa	1.6	285	3.7	62	0.05	66	1.16	10
Republic of Korea	4.7	103	11.4	25	0.08	37	1.46	8
Türkiye	1.4	421	7.6	41	0.06	59	1.40	10
United Kingdom	6.9	74	11.5	27	0.12	9	1.72	8
United States	2.4	220	4.4	69	0.07	23	0.83	16
Simple Average	**3.7**	**171**	**7.8**	**51**	**0.11**	**39**	**1.19**	**14**

GJ = gigajoule, kWh = kilowatt-hour, PRC = People's Republic of China.

Note: Baseline prices from 2018.

Source: International Monetary Fund.

Some European countries have opted to reduce tax rates, offering a flat rate reduction for emission-intensive industries or granting a free basic allowance while taxing emissions only at the margin.

Reduced tax liability constitutes state aid, and EU guidelines on state aid for environmental protection say that the reductions cannot exceed 80% unless binding agreements with the government ensure that emission reductions correspond to what would be achieved at 20% of the tax rate. Any such reductions are time-bound to a maximum of 10 years and subject to annual controls. Energy-intensive industries are defined as entities whose purchases of energy products amount to at least 3% of production value (EUR-Lex 2003). As such, energy-intensive trade-exposed sectors are frequently allowed to phase in the full carbon tax gradually.

Cement is one industry that frequently lobbies for carbon tax exemption to accommodate its reliance on coal for clinker. Cement is energy-intensive but typically consumed locally because it is expensive to transport relative to its value, leaving it only moderately exposed to foreign competition (Fitz Gerald et al. 2009). Considering significant emissions of about 1 ton of CO_2 per ton of cement, it is important to provide economic stimulus to reduce emissions, which may prompt the construction industry to substitute away from concrete with other building materials.

Only sustainable biofuels should be allowed full carbon tax rate reductions, while biofuels made from wastes and nonfood second-generation cellulosic material may deserve a full exemption when carbon tax has been paid on their previous uses.

7. Determine compensation to low-income households.

A statistical institute study in India has shown fuel taxes imposing a higher relative burden on the rich than the poor, except in relation to kerosene used to light homes and for cooking (Datta 2010). By recycling some of the revenue as targeted compensation for poor households, it is possible to maintain incentives to reduce the consumption of carbon-intensive fuels. Tax experts recommend targeted tax credits paid out through an annual tax declaration procedure, so that households identified as low-income receive compensation as a guaranteed and income-graduated credit against the taxes due—as a green bonus (OECD 2002).

Other options where low-income and poor households, such as subsistence farmers, need not file taxes annually include cash transfers and transfers in kind such as the provision of health care; education; social security; or public infrastructure, including public transportation. Some countries use block-pricing schemes for electricity, allowing a specified amount of consumption at a reduced rate. A disadvantage of this is that all consumers benefit, not only low-income households, making it a very expensive way to compensate. Studies in Latin America have shown that applying subsidies across the board raises the cost of compensating the poorest quintile by an order of magnitude. In contrast, only a smaller fraction of revenue from carbon taxation, about 8%–10%, is needed to compensate the bottom quintile of poor and vulnerable households because poorer households consume less fossil fuel than others for transportation and heating (Feng et al. 2018). Cash transfers have far lower transaction costs than other methods. Suggestions for country-specific cash transfers to compensate for carbon taxation have been made by the IMF (Alonso and Kilpatrick 2022).

8. Assess macroeconomic impacts.

Carbon taxation differs from a simple increase of energy prices in that all revenue remains within the domestic economy. Conventional wisdom in the economics literature is that proceeds from carbon taxation should be recycled to lower income and payroll taxes while aiming for revenue neutrality (Tol et al. 2008; Keseljevic and Koman 2015; Pereira, Pereira, and Rodrigues 2016). Such schemes stimulate employment while providing incentives for energy efficiency and low-carbon energy (Barker et al. 2009). They have frequently been shown to be superior to reducing value-added or capital taxes, for instance, and compared to increasing the tax burden by claiming revenue for the general budget (Seixas et al. 2017). Further stimulus to employment comes from diverting demand from imported fuel to domestic supply, relieving the balance of payments. It depends, however, on context and the specifics of the recycling mechanisms whether a double dividend in terms of a long-term stimulus to economic growth will accrue from carbon taxation (Pearce 1991, Goulder 1995, Jaeger 2012). Carbon taxation affects households' living costs and businesses' factor costs both directly and indirectly; aside from the energy cost increase per se, also passed on are higher costs for numerous other products, including food. Balancing revenue recycling mechanisms between households and companies requires great care.

In some OECD countries, income tax reductions aim to support households, while reductions in payroll taxes paid by employers aim to support businesses. Emerging and developing economies need to consider additional measures to ensure a just transition. The poorest segments of the population, who are often not liable to income taxes, could for instance benefit from direct support for electrification to allow them to substitute away from kerosene and fuelwood. Energy-intensive companies using outdated and inefficient technology could benefit from investment tax credits and technological advisory services. Earmarking 10%–20% of revenue to co-fund low-carbon technology implementation in industry can support a faster transformation (Andersen 2010). Carbon tax revenue can be used to fund research and development programs to develop novel green technologies while strengthening collaboration between university and company research. Macroeconomic modeling can project the impacts of different revenue-recycling mechanisms.

Environmentalists frequently argue that proceeds from carbon taxes should be earmarked for climate change mitigation. However, earmarking introduces rigidity in public budgets and is often disallowed. Most OECD countries with carbon taxes channel revenue into their general budget (Table 5). Nevertheless, even if the revenue flows into the general budget, it is still possible to make disbursements for climate change mitigation or to allocate money for revolving funds.

9. Determine institutional oversight.

Environmental authorities are typically charged with developing NDCs and have in a few countries assumed responsibility for administrating the collection of carbon taxes in light of their access to data on company emissions. However, environmental authorities frequently do not have the compliance and enforcement expertise and procedures that tax authorities have developed over the years. Successful carbon taxation schemes require constructive collaboration between environmental and tax authorities.

Table 5: Use of Carbon Tax Revenue by OECD Countries (%)

Country	Environmental Spending	Revenue Recycling	General Budget
Canada	10	90	0
Chile	0	0	100
Denmark	0	0	100
Finland	0	0	100
France	27	0	73
Iceland	0	0	100
Ireland	0	0	100
Japan	100	0	0
Norway	0	0	100
Portugal	36	0	64
Slovenia	0	0	100
Sweden	0	0	100
Switzerland	26	74	0
UK	0	0	100

OECD = Organisation for Economic Co-operation and Development, UK = United Kingdom.
Source: Yunis and Aliakbari 2020.

Tax authorities should be center stage in any carbon tax scheme, but environmental authorities can provide support, such as by providing data on indirect emissions, the waste sector, industrial F-gases, and emissions from flaring at domestic oil and gas fields. When fossil fuels are taxed at the point of import or production, company data on fossil fuel use does not have to be reported for tax purposes. The timing of carbon tax installments can follow other regular procedures, such as for value-added tax, to allow sufficient business cycle liquidity. Reporting procedures should be coordinated with environmental authorities, which need the same data for the emission inventories used to prepare NDCs. Digital bookkeeping and submission are strongly recommended. Failure to register and report should be subject to routine compliance mechanisms on tax evasion.

10. Establish monitoring for ex-post evaluation.

To improve understanding of how carbon taxation affects households and companies, it is advisable to build in a framework for ex-post evaluation. The framework will inform data needs and responsibilities for data collection, while allocating sufficient resources for collection. Baseline data on emissions immediately prior to the carbon tax needs to be secured and disaggregated by sector.

11. Consult stakeholders.

Green tax commissions with experts from different ministries, research institutes, and universities have frequently offered support to governments during carbon tax preparation. Such commissions are well placed to consult with different stakeholders, understand their mitigation options, and prepare economic modeling studies to simulate impacts on emissions, vulnerable households, and business sectors, as well as to provide authoritative forecasts of macroeconomic implications. They require at least 1–2 years to complete their tasks. Considering the urgency of curbing GHG emissions and potential disruption from phasing in carbon taxation too abruptly, Singapore offers a good example to follow (Figure 10 and section below). Singapore launched its carbon tax with an introductory rate while awaiting commission deliberations on a trajectory toward 2030 and suggestions for appropriate compensation mechanisms. In addition to economic and legal advice, such commissions require expertise on low-carbon technology and behavioral response.

C. Learning from Existing Carbon Taxes in Emerging Economies

It is worthwhile to consider the carbon taxation experience in several countries.

Uruguay transformed, in 2022, its preexisting excise tax by aligning the tax rate strictly to carbon content (Twidale 2022, Sartori 2021, Surtidores.uy 2022). The carbon tax rate of $127 per ton of CO_2 addresses motor fuels. Electricity is generated almost entirely from renewables. As there was no overall increase in the tax burden, revenue continues to accrue to the general budget, which will shoulder the costs of meeting NDC targets.

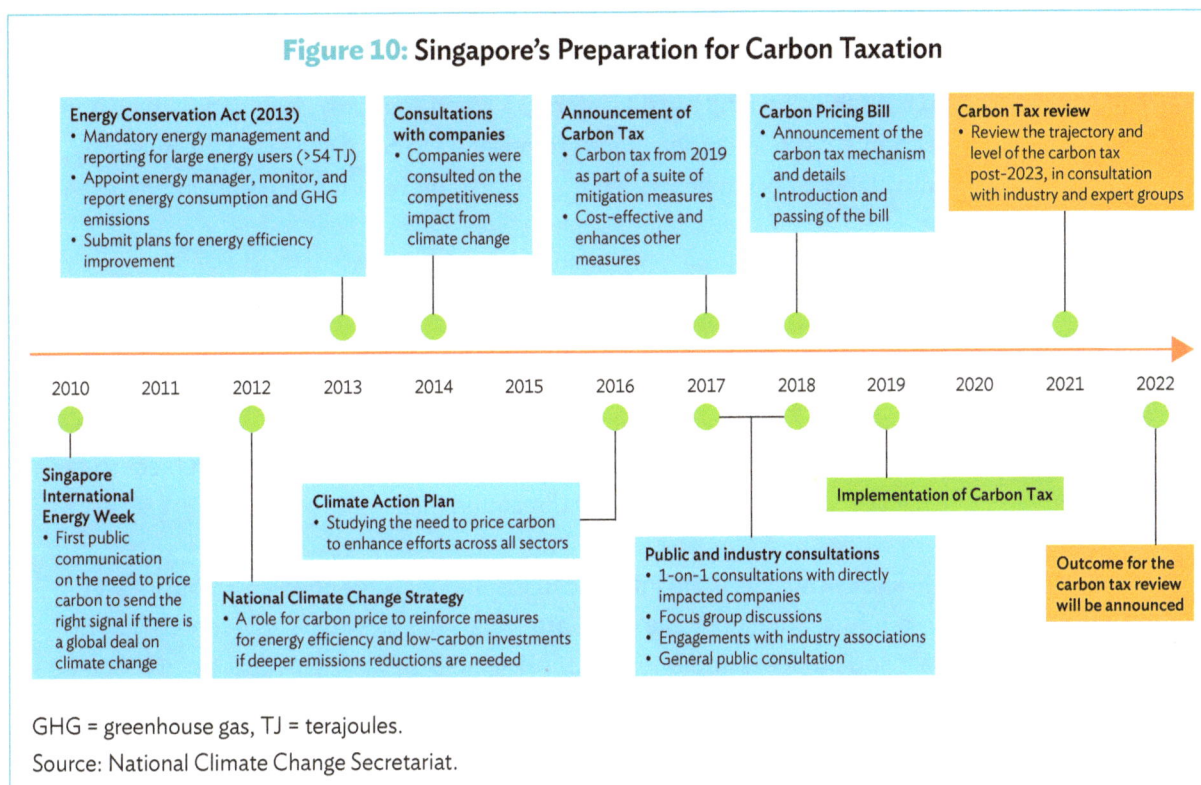

Figure 10: Singapore's Preparation for Carbon Taxation

Energy Conservation Act (2013)
- Mandatory energy management and reporting for large energy users (>54 TJ)
- Appoint energy manager, monitor, and report energy consumption and GHG emissions
- Submit plans for energy efficiency improvement

Consultations with companies
- Companies were consulted on the competitiveness impact from climate change

Announcement of Carbon Tax
- Carbon tax from 2019 as part of a suite of mitigation measures
- Cost-effective and enhances other measures

Carbon Pricing Bill
- Announcement of the carbon tax mechanism and details
- Introduction and passing of the bill

Carbon Tax review
- Review the trajectory and level of the carbon tax post-2023, in consultation with industry and expert groups

2010 2011 2012 2013 2014 2015 2016 2017 2018 2019 2020 2021 2022

Singapore International Energy Week
- First public communication on the need to price carbon to send the right signal if there is a global deal on climate change

National Climate Change Strategy
- A role for carbon price to reinforce measures for energy efficiency and low-carbon investments if deeper emissions reductions are needed

Climate Action Plan
- Studying the need to price carbon to enhance efforts across all sectors

Public and industry consultations
- 1-on-1 consultations with directly impacted companies
- Focus group discussions
- Engagements with industry associations
- General public consultation

Implementation of Carbon Tax

Outcome for the carbon tax review will be announced

GHG = greenhouse gas, TJ = terajoules.
Source: National Climate Change Secretariat.

In 2017, Colombia implemented a carbon tax on fossil fuels at a rate of $5 per ton of CO_2, expecting it to deliver 7% of the NDC (Pinzón Téllez 2019, Fonseca-Gómez 2018). Revenue accrues to a national fund, providing support for rural and environmental projects. Carbon tax liability can be offset with certificates from the voluntary carbon market, most of which stem from forestry projects to slow deforestation and protect biodiversity. This option has been popular with the largest emitters, considerably eroding revenue generation for the fund.

In 2019, South Africa implemented a carbon tax on fossil fuels with a rate that has reached $9 per ton of CO_2. In one of the most coal-reliant economies in the world, power plants and industries benefit from reductions and exemptions in the initial phase. The carbon tax is imposed directly on emitters, for industry on 40% of emissions, though an emitter may reduce tax liability by a further 10% through carbon credits bought on the voluntary market. There are additional deductions: 10% for process and fugitive emissions, 10% for trade-exposed sectors, and 5% for firms with lower emission intensity. The carbon tax rate will escalate by at least $1 per ton annually to reach $30 by 2030 (Steenkamp 2022; Deloitte, n.d.).

Ukraine has taxed carbon since 2016, with a rate that reached $0.33 per ton of CO_2 in 2019. The tax covers all stationary sources, including power plants, metals, chemicals, and food, but the rate is too low to incentivize energy savings or fuel shifting. It is part of an environmental tax code, and lack of proper accounting procedures is considered to have enabled tax evasion. However, increasing the tax rate to a modest $3.50 per ton of CO_2 could reduce Ukraine's emissions by 10%, according to a detailed modeling study (Frey 2017, Breuing 2020).

Singapore implemented a carbon tax in 2019 at a rate of $3.60 and plans to increase it to $18 in 2024, with a view to reaching $36–$58 in 2030. The revenue will be used to support decarbonization efforts and to cushion businesses and households during the transition to a green economy. Companies may, from 2024, surrender high-quality international carbon credits to offset up to 5% of their taxable emissions. Consultations continue with stakeholders to ensure a transitional framework for emission-intensive and trade-exposed companies (NCCS 2002).

D. Risks and Concerns

An appropriate policy to mitigate climate change that is also financially sound requires, in addition to carbon pricing, that fossil fuel subsidies be terminated. Moreover, motor fuels should be subject to excise taxes sufficient to match the cost of road construction and maintenance.

However, if subsidy reform and tax increases are introduced too suddenly for people and businesses to adjust, discontent may spur fuel protests (Table 6). If, after years of passivity, a government lumps together all at once several good purposes into one abrupt price increase for fossil fuels, an unprepared population can be expected to react. Numerous past examples show that badly prepared price or tax hikes can cause riots and sometimes even bloody conflicts.

Table 6: Policy Process toward Carbon Taxation

→ Announce policy intention to aim for a price on carbon.
→ Request experts to identify a role for its carbon tax in mitigation strategy.
→ Receive first input from business and labor unions on implications.
→ Prepare legal and institutional frameworks for a carbon tax.
→ Analyze tax rates and trajectories for increase over time.
→ Identify impacts on low-income households and compensation mechanisms.
→ Identify impacts on energy intensive and trade-exposed industries.
→ Determine accompanying measures to smooth implementation.
→ Conduct public consultation, including on revenue-recycling options.
→ Agree on and announce the implementation date for the carbon tax.

Source: Authors.

In the winter of 2021–2022, Kazakhstan suffered fuel protests when a price cap on liquefied petroleum gas (LPG) for motor fuel was removed, doubling the pump price to motorists within days. However, under the price cap, LPG was being sold below production cost and at half the price in some neighbor countries, encouraging illegal exports and causing chronic shortages of LPG within Kazakhstan itself. The price cap had to be reintroduced to satisfy protesters (Kumenov and Lillis 2022).

Such revolts in opposition to fuel price rises are always triggered by a relative increase of 30% or more, while the absolute increase plays a lesser role. In Kazakhstan, the 100% increase took a liter of LPG from $0.12 to $0.24.

Some experts advise that, in developing countries, no motor fuel price increase should exceed 10% of the end-user price, for reasons of mass psychology (Metschies 1999). Instead, numerous, regularly spaced but modest price increases are recommended, including an annual adjustment according to the consumer price index. As energy prices are settled on the international market, currency fluctuations can complicate matters. The 14 countries of the African Financial Community Franc Zone on one occasion saw the value of their currency slashed by half but, through incremental adjustments, nevertheless managed to adjust fuel prices to the new exchange rate step by step.

The intricate interplay of currency rates and international energy markets suggests that, in times of large fluctuations in international energy prices, annual consumer price index adjustments to excises and carbon tax rates should be done according to the core consumer price index, thus excluding energy prices, to facilitate adaptation.

E. European Union's Carbon Border Adjustment Mechanism

Carbon pricing payments in Asia and the Pacific will be rebated on exports into the EU under the Carbon Border Adjustment Mechanism (CBAM) about to be implemented (EUR-Lex 2021).

As the EU ETS since 2005 prices carbon emissions from large power plants and industries, a corresponding carbon price will, from 2026, be levied on products sold into the European market. A carbon price will be placed on energy-intensive products from outside the EU: aluminum, iron and steel, cement, fertilizers, and electricity. Coverage will be extended once the technical issues of including additional sectors, such as in chemicals, have been sorted out. The EU carbon price fluctuated in 2022 from €65 to €98 per ton of CO_2.

Rationale. The CBAM will allow the EU to phase out the granting of free allowances in its trade-exposed sectors. Gradually, a higher share of the annual allowances will be auctioned, raising the cost of emitting carbon and strengthening the case for developing and adopting cleaner technologies using low-carbon energy sources. These energy-intensive industries currently receive free allowances based on a benchmark corresponding to the best-performing decile of firms in each sector. At the sector level, the CBAM brings a shift from free allowances covering about half the emissions to full auctioning by 2036.

Mechanisms. The CBAM will begin operating in 2023, with the first payments due in 2026. Suppliers to the European market are expected to declare their CO_2 emissions and purchase emission certificates corresponding to the share of emissions embodied in their products (Figure 11). Certificates will be priced to reflect the carbon price within the EU. Declarations will undergo verification checks. Should producers be unable to declare their actual emissions, default values will be applied corresponding to the average emission intensity for the goods and country in question. Where countries cannot provide reliable data, the default value will be derived from the 10% worst-performing installations in the EU for those types of goods.

Figure 11: European Union Carbon Border Adjustment Mechanism

EU importers of goods covered by the CBAM registers with national authorities where they can also buy **CBAM certificates.** Certificates are priced based on **weekly ETS allowances.**

EU importer **declares the emissions** embedded in its imports and **surrenders** the corresponding number of certificates each year.

If importers can prove that a **carbon price has already been paid** during the production of the imported goods, the corresponding amount **can be deducted.**

CBAM = European Union Carbon Border Adjustment Mechanism, ETS = emission trading system, EU = European Union.
Source: European Commission.

Where a supplier from outside the EU has paid a carbon price in the country of origin, whether as a carbon tax or to acquire an emission allowance, this payment can be offset against the requirement to hold emission certificates corresponding to the emissions embodied in products. However, excises and other taxes levied on different tax bases than carbon are not eligible, and any export rebates or compensations provided by the country of origin will be deducted.

Implications. With the CBAM, the EU aims to level up mitigation efforts on a high but level playing field while respecting the rules of the World Trade Organization. Hence, the EU will not refund the carbon tax on its exports outside of the EU, as this would jeopardize CBAM compliance with World Trade Organization rules. Revenue accruing from the CBAM will be used to underpin mitigation. In accordance with the principle of common but differentiated responsibilities under the UNFCCC, the EU plans to recycle some CBAM revenue to support adaptation and mitigation efforts in least-developed countries.

As India and the PRC both have large exports to the EU from affected sectors, a carbon certificate price of €80 per ton of CO_2 implies an increase by up to 190% in the cost of using coal. As natural gas has lower carbon content, its energy costs will increase by up to 110% relative to domestic market prices in 2021. However, the certificate carbon price will increase only gradually to the full rate, in tandem with phasing out free allowances by 2036 in those sectors. Firms in the PRC may be able to obtain reductions on carbon emission allowance payments under the country's ETS, while Indian firms will not be able to deduct their coal tax payments unless the tax base explicitly refers to carbon contents. The CBAM will apply to imports from anywhere outside of the EU, presumably with some exemptions for least-developed countries (Figure 12).

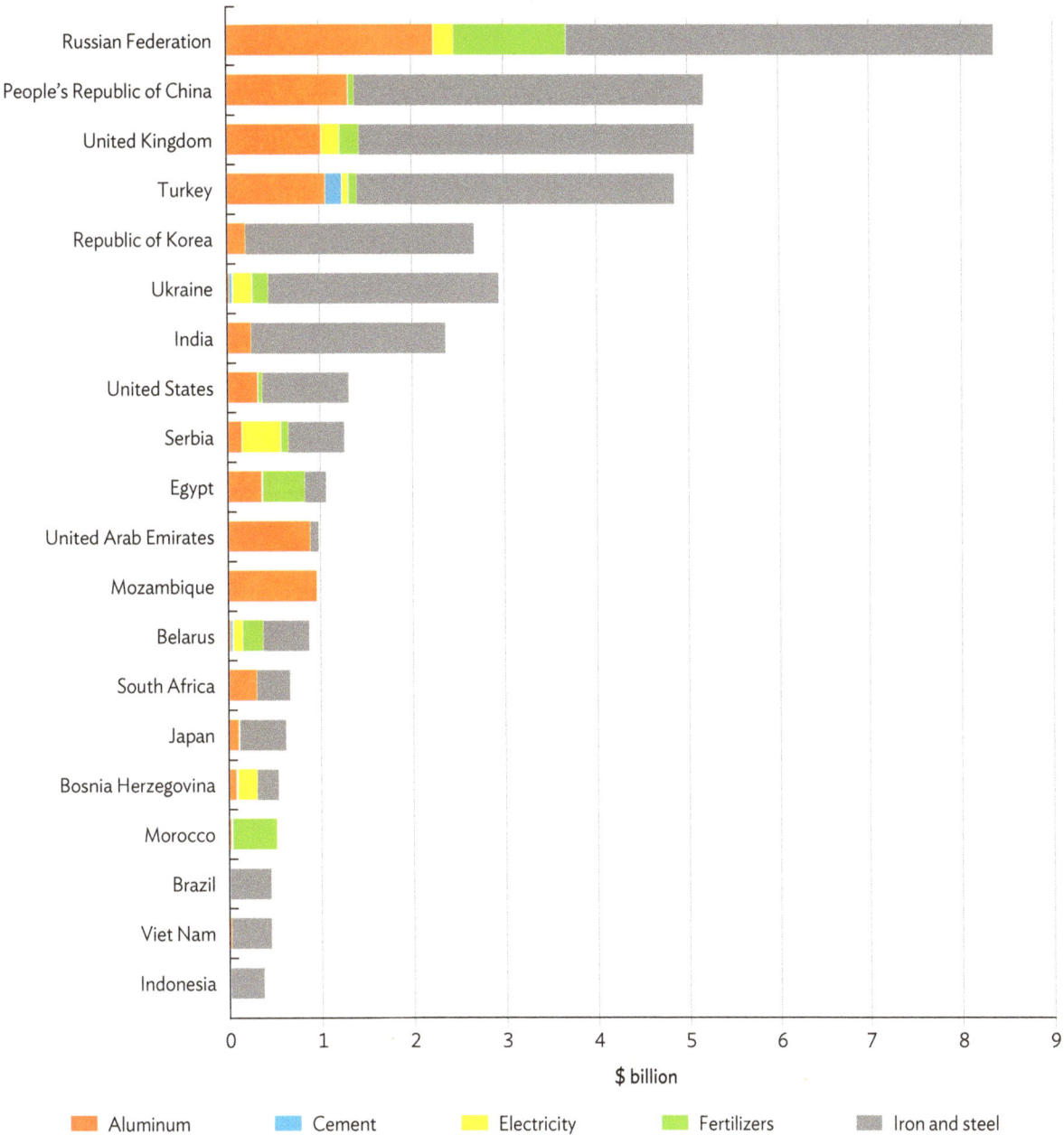

Figure 12: Top 20 Exporters to the European Union of Carbon Border Adjustment Mechanism Goods

Source: Knoema. 2021. International Carbon Tax: Who Will Pay for the EU's Green Future? https://knoema.com/infographics/pgtukpc/international-carbon-tax-who-will-pay-for-the-eu-s-green-future.

The theoretical benefits of fossil fuel subsidy rationalization (FFSR) are well known (Figure 13). In practice, however, governments encounter a wide range of obstacles—political, economic, and social—when attempting to reform fossil fuel subsidies (FFSs). These obstacles often manifest as strong opposition from key interest groups in extractive, electric power, and energy-intensive manufacturing sectors, and as protests sparked by anticipated negative social impacts.

Figure 13: Benefits of Fossil Fuel Subsidy Rationalization

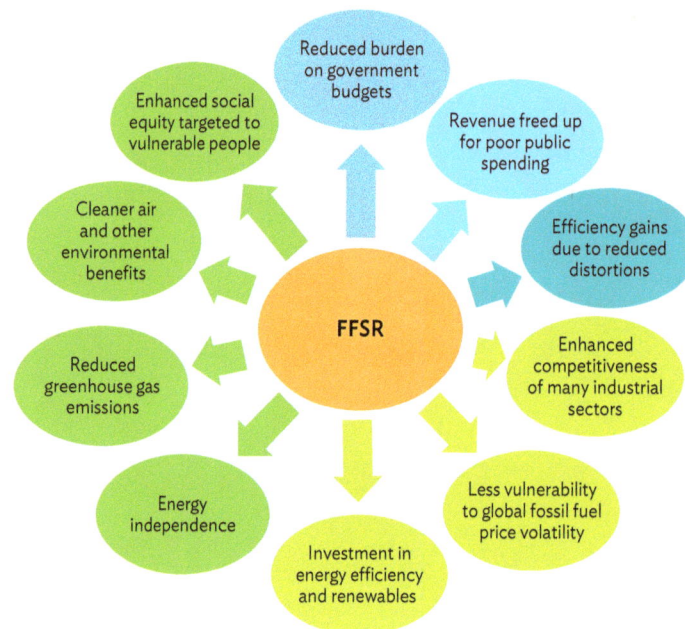

FFSR = fossil fuel subsidy rationalization.
Source: Authors.

A. Objectives and Purpose of This Step-by-Step Guide

To address obstacles to FFSR effectively, governments must approach the issue strategically and build a broad political and societal consensus in favor of rationalization within government, across key stakeholders, and among the general public. This step-by-step guide was written with policymakers in Asian Development Bank (ADB) developing member countries (DMCs) in mind. It delineates a series of analytical and practical steps to tackle the political challenges of rationalization and develop a strategy that can successfully and permanently eliminate FFSs. The guide is structured by a series of steps, as shown in Figure 14.

Figure 14: **Steps in the Preparation and Strategic Design of a Rationalization Strategy**

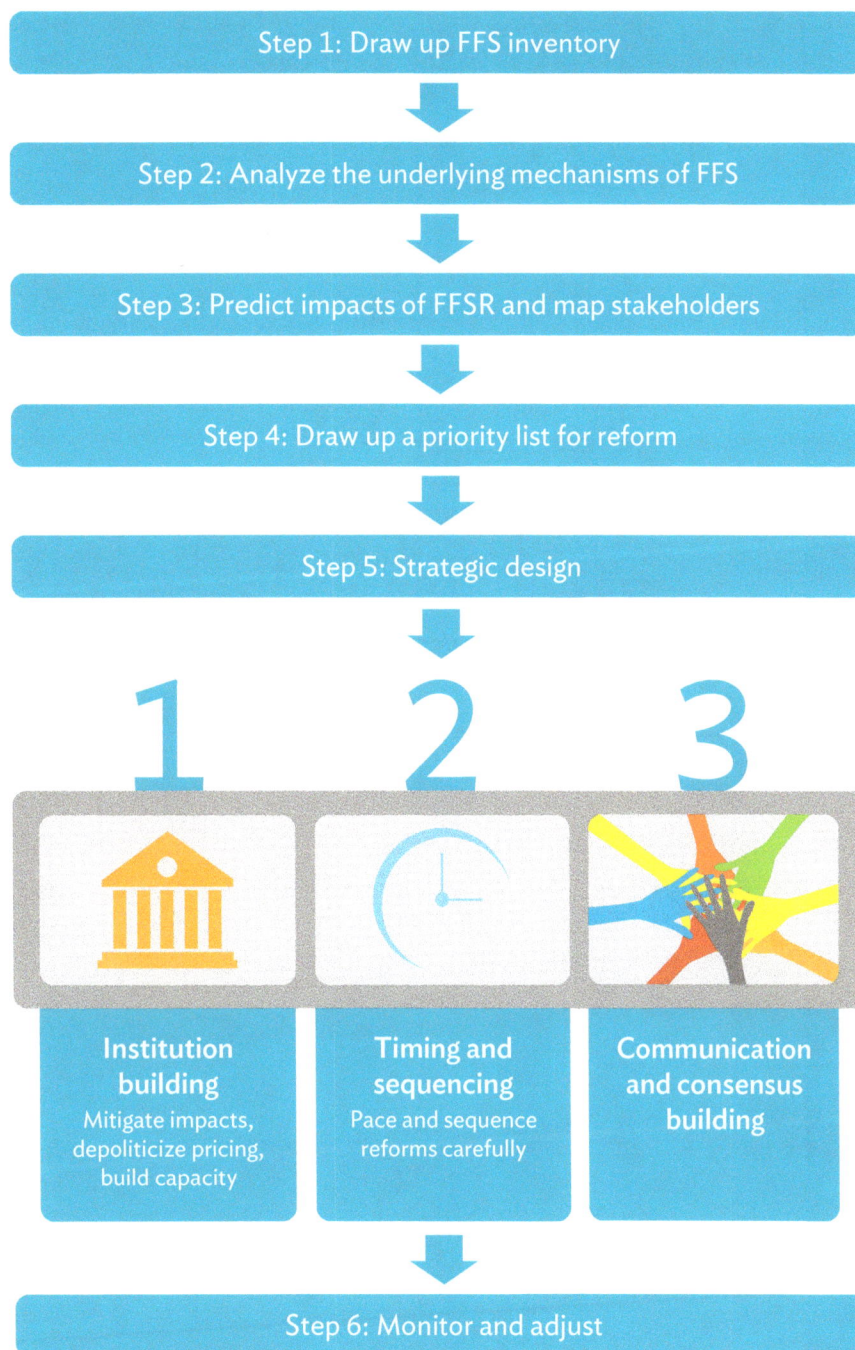

Step 1: Draw up FFS inventory

Step 2: Analyze the underlying mechanisms of FFS

Step 3: Predict impacts of FFSR and map stakeholders

Step 4: Draw up a priority list for reform

Step 5: Strategic design

1

2

3

Institution building

Mitigate impacts, depoliticize pricing, build capacity

Timing and sequencing

Pace and sequence reforms carefully

Communication and consensus building

Step 6: Monitor and adjust

FFS = fossil fuel subsidy, FFSR = fossil fuel subsidy rationalization.

Sources: Authors, drawing on C. Beaton et al. 2013. *A Guide to Fossil Fuel Subsidy Reform for Policy-Makers in South East Asia.* Geneva: International Institute for Sustainable Development/Global Subsidies Initiative. https://www.iisd.org/gsi/sites/default/files/ffs_guidebook.pdf; B. Clements et al., eds. 2013. *Energy Subsidy Reform: Lessons and Implications.* Washington, DC: International Monetary Fund. https://www.imf.org/en/Publications/Policy-Papers/Issues/2016/12/31/Energy-Subsidy-Reform-Lessons-and-Implications-PP4741; and OECD. 2021. *OECD Companion to the Inventory of Support Measures for Fossil Fuels 2021.* Paris: Organisation for Economic Co-operation and Development. https://doi.org/10.1787/e670c620-en.

B. Step-by-Step Guide to Rationalizing Fossil Fuel Subsidies

FFSR requires a whole-economy approach and careful consideration of potential adverse effects, particularly on distribution and competitiveness. Careful groundwork is required to prevent policy reversals and inform and facilitate the design of a successful process. This preparatory stage to gather and analyze data is vital, as a lack of information regarding the magnitude and shortcomings of FFSs is a major barrier to successful FFSR.

1. Draw up an inventory of fossil fuel subsidies.

It is good practice in public financial governance to enhance transparency in government expenditure and to generate as much data and information as possible to inform budgetary decision-making. This enhances public understanding of environmentally friendly and environmentally harmful expenditures and other government actions, including FFSs.

Drawing up a subsidy inventory can stimulate debate and raise awareness of the comparative size of FFSs. Drawing up an FFS inventory is an important exercise for all ADB DMCs, whether or not governments have concrete plans or commitments to FFSR, and it is often a critical first step toward receiving ADB climate change policy-based loans. Box 22 describes Germany's biannual subsidy report.

When drawing up an inventory, the first challenge DMCs face is defining an FFS. A good starting point is the International Energy Agency (IEA) definition of an energy subsidy: any government action that primarily concerns the energy sector and lowers the cost of energy production, raises the price received by energy producers, or lowers the price paid by energy consumers (IEA 1999). Within this definition, there are several key points for policymakers to consider: (i) Subsidies can be paid to consumers and energy producers. (ii) FFSs can apply at all stages along the value chain, from extraction to consumption. (iii) Any government action can be considered a subsidy—not just explicit transfers, but also implicit support and transfers of risk. Figure 15 illustrates this complexity.

Box 22

Reporting on State Aid and Tax Concessions in Germany

The German Ministry of Finance has reported on state aid and tax concessions since 1967, fine-tuning and improving the report over time. Today, the report includes a sustainability impact assessment conducted for all subsidies. Reporting brings transparency into the public domain, stimulates debate, and raises awareness of comparative amounts of fossil fuel subsidies and other measures. It is an important source of information as the government and Parliament review existing subsidies.

The government has developed subsidy policy guidelines to prevent new subsidies from locking in and to ensure that all subsidies are efficient; time-limited; and subject to regular evaluation in terms of target attainment, efficiency, and transparency.

Source: Government of Germany, Federal Ministry of Finance. 2022. *28th Subsidy Report: 2019–2022*. https://www.bundesfinanzministerium.de/Content/EN/Standardartikel/Press_Room/Publications/Brochures/28-subsidy-report.pdf?__blob=publicationFile&v=2.

Figure 15: Typology of Fossil Fuel Subsidies

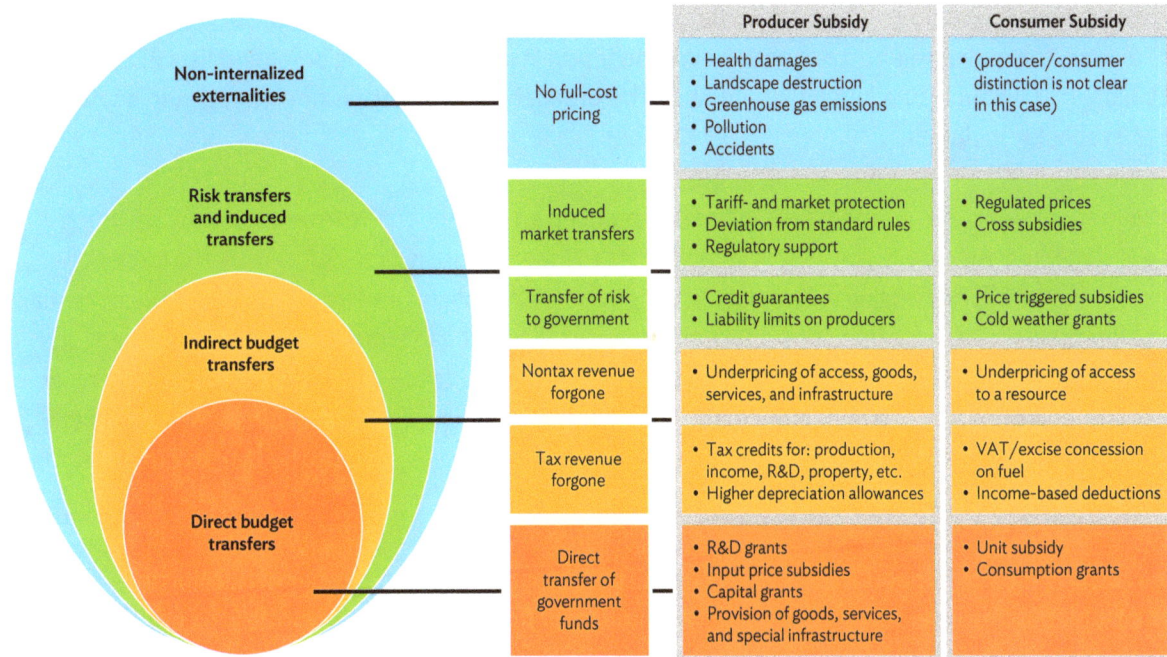

		Producer Subsidy	Consumer Subsidy
Non-internalized externalities	No full-cost pricing	• Health damages • Landscape destruction • Greenhouse gas emissions • Pollution • Accidents	• (producer/consumer distinction is not clear in this case)
Risk transfers and induced transfers	Induced market transfers	• Tariff- and market protection • Deviation from standard rules • Regulatory support	• Regulated prices • Cross subsidies
	Transfer of risk to government	• Credit guarantees • Liability limits on producers	• Price triggered subsidies • Cold weather grants
Indirect budget transfers	Nontax revenue forgone	• Underpricing of access, goods, services, and infrastructure	• Underpricing of access to a resource
	Tax revenue forgone	• Tax credits for: production, income, R&D, property, etc. • Higher depreciation allowances	• VAT/excise concession on fuel • Income-based deductions
Direct budget transfers	Direct transfer of government funds	• R&D grants • Input price subsidies • Capital grants • Provision of goods, services, and special infrastructure	• Unit subsidy • Consumption grants

R&D = research and development, VAT = value-added tax.

Source: C. Adolf et al. 2014. *TTIP and Fossil Fuel Subsidies: Using International Policy Processes as Entry Points for Reform in the EU and the USA.* Heinrich Boell Stiftung TTIP Series. https://eu.boell.org/sites/default/files/hbs_ttip_fossil_fuel_subsidies_1.pdf.

Initially, governments may focus on specific types of FFS, expanding in subsequent iterations the coverage and scope of the screening process. DMCs with scarce human and technical capacity, in particular, may find it helpful to focus on FFSs for which data are already available, such as transfers or tax expenditures in budgetary reporting. Such an approach would focus on the types of subsidy shown in the lower two circles in Figure 15, direct and indirect budget transfers, and within these two categories, focus on direct transfers of government funds and tax revenue forgone. DMC governments should consider both consumer and producer subsidies, as both can be large.

An initial inventory should aim to include subsidies with the highest impact in terms of both burden on public budgets and harmful impacts on the climate, the environment, or human health. In DMCs with regulated fossil fuel prices, this means looking at a specific example of the third category of subsidies: induced market transfers, typically from direct price regulation, pricing formulas, border controls or taxes, and domestic purchase and supply mandates (UNEP 2019, Annex 3). The price gap approach can be used to quantify these subsidies.[7]

---

[7] To generate comparable data between countries on FFSs, both the IMF and the IEA use a price gap approach, which compares average end-user prices paid by consumers in the country to a benchmark price reflecting the full cost of supply: the cost of fossil fuels, their internal distribution, and any value-added tax. It is summarized in this equation:

consumer price support = (benchmark price/unit – local net-of-tax price/unit) x units subsidized

For a detailed explanation, see IEA (2022) and UNEP (2019), p. 38.

An example of a relatively limited approach can be found in Indonesia's voluntary self-report on FFSs in the Group of Twenty peer review process, which identified just 12 FFSs: five direct budgetary transfers and seven tax expenditures. Although some types of subsidy were not considered, such as preferential tax treatment or government credit assistance, the report is a useful starting point and lists FFSs worth $9 billion in 2016. In future iterations, scope can be broadened, the process fine-tuned, and additional types of subsidy included.

In the medium term, governments should aim to build up a comprehensive inventory of FFSs, which entails screening regulations, programs, and policies to identify subsidy measures in all the circles shown in Figure 15, drawing up a complete list of government policies and programs that have potential to preferentially treat or benefit consumers or producers. The list can subsequently be populated with additional information: subsidy estimates, beneficiaries, incidence, etc. This thorough screening of policies and programs can help bring to light off-budget subsidies. The largest circle, which looks at uninternalized externalities, can be informed by the methodologies used by the IMF to quantify post-tax subsidies (IMF 2022).

The OECD Matrix of Support Measures is a useful guide for this exercise (Appendix). Ministry staff tasked with completing the inventory—typically in the ministry of finance or economy, often in cooperation with the ministry of environment—can also draw on the OECD inventory of fossil fuel support measures for examples of subsidies under each transfer mechanism.[8]

An inventory should quantify identified subsidies to the extent that this is possible. Quantifying subsidies is relatively simple for direct transfers, as these figures are readily available in annual budgetary statements. Estimating other types of support calls for measuring the difference between applied tax rates, regulated prices, interest rates, and realized equity return and their reference counterparts. A United Nations Environment Programme guide on measuring FFSs provides methodologies for this process (UNEP 2019).

To maximize positive outcomes from drawing up an FFS inventory, DMC governments may wish to access international support, through either the online Sustainable Development Goal 12 Hub, which is open to all countries, or through participation in voluntary FFS self-reporting and peer review processes established under the auspices of the Group of Twenty and Asia-Pacific Economic Cooperation (Box 23). To pave the way for a long-term process of subsidy rationalization, DMC governments should consider introducing regular subsidy reports every 2–3 years to sustain the conversation, raise awareness, and improve transparency.

---

[8]   The methodology used, including a glossary of support mechanisms and beneficiaries, is found in OECD (n.d.). Examples of each type of subsidy can be found in the OECD database.

Box 23

Accessing International Support: Sustainable Development Goal 12 Hub and Voluntary Peer Review

Sustainable Development Goal (SDG) target 12.C calls on countries to "rationalize inefficient fossil fuel subsidies that encourage wasteful consumption by removing market distortions." The SDG 12 Hub is an interagency collaboration that supports the efforts of all countries to streamline methodologies and processes to achieve SDG 12. It aims to be a one-stop shop for governments, businesses, civil society, and the public for tracking and reporting on progress. The hub offers direct access to data, guidance, capacity building, and official reporting, and it facilitates the sharing of progress, knowledge, and solutions.

The Asia-Pacific Economic Cooperation (APEC) and the Group of Twenty have developed and implemented peer reviews of voluntary self-reporting of fossil fuel subsidies (FFSs). Countries work in pairs to peer review each other's self-report on FFSs with support from international experts. Asian Development Bank developing member countries Indonesia and the Philippines have participated, and India is planning a peer review with France. Participating countries agree on specific objectives for the exchange, typically sharing lessons and experiences of subsidy inventories and rationalization. The process has been an important in-country learning experience across ministries and has become a means of facilitating knowledge exchange and building capacity to design reform. Peer reviews contain many useful recommendations for participating governments and reference best practice and successful examples from similar countries. Reviews have set precedents on the structure and conduct of FFS inventories and the coverage of measures discussed. Detailed lessons learned can be found in OECD (2022).

Sources: SDG 12 Hub. https://sdg12hub.org; OECD. 2022. Lessons Learnt and Good Practice from APEC-Economy Fossil-Fuel Subsidy Peer Reviews. *OECD Environment Policy Paper*. No. 29. Contribution by the OECD to the APEC Energy Working Group, July 2021. Paris: Organisation for Economic Co-operation and Development. https://doi.org/10.1787/63ba96a5-en.

2. Analyze the underlying mechanisms of fossil fuel subsidies.

Once a subsidy inventory has been drawn up, it is necessary to build an understanding of the underlying mechanisms of FFSs. This can help DMC governments have a clearer picture of how subsidies operate and affect the price of fossil fuels, and to understand the extent to which international fossil fuel prices are passed through to consumers. However, even full pass-through of international fossil fuel prices in domestic markets does not imply the rationalization of all FFSs; implicit and explicit subsidies for producers and consumers may still exist in the form of depreciation allowances, tax credits for producers, underpricing of access to infrastructure, or value-added tax concessions. Nonetheless, allowing pass-through of prices to domestic markets is an important step in the right direction, as it creates price signals in favor of more efficient fossil fuel use and fuel shifting to low-carbon energy sources.

DMC governments can analyze FFSs along the four dimensions of fuel pricing explained in Table 7. Answering the questions in the left-hand column develops a clear picture of how FFSs function in the economy, and how prices are affected by them. Responses should be used to inform the preparatory and subsequent strategic design process.

Table 7: **Four Dimensions of Fossil Fuel Pricing**

Questions for DMCs	Explanation
Fossil fuel price regulation What mechanisms currently influence fossil fuel prices? How do they influence prices? Do they limit the pass-through of price fluctuation to consumers?	In DMCs, FFS often take the form of regulated prices, either through ad hoc price regulation, in which case prices are set arbitrarily and pass-through is limited, or active regulation, which places constraints on pass-through to smooth out global price volatility. If energy markets are not regulated but liberalized and competitive, price rises will be passed on to consumers.
Level of subsidies and/or taxation How much do FFSs reduce fossil fuel prices for end users? What is the incidence of the subsidy, i.e., what aspect of production or consumption does it target? How are fossil fuels taxed and to what extent?	Policymakers should try to understand the underlying mechanisms of FFSs, the extent of price pass-through to consumers, and their incidence in the supply chain. Where fossil fuel taxes exist, the analysis should establish whether low or high rates of taxation exist by drawing on International Monetary Fund data on post-tax subsidies, for example, or using international benchmarks.
Transparency To what extent is the composition and regulation of energy prices open and transparent?	Ultimately, the aim of DMC governments should be for fossil fuel pricing to be fully transparent and depoliticized, with data on fuel price composition, pricing mechanisms, and government decision-making in the public domain. Identifying where this is not the case can highlight priorities for reform.
Enforcement To what degree is energy pricing monitored, supervised, and enforced?	DMC governments should aim to ensure that fair competition prevents monopolistically high energy prices or collusion of suppliers and establish whether predatory pricing, smuggling, black markets, or fuel adulteration are issues that should be tackled during FFS rationalization.

DMC = developing member country, FFS = fossil fuel subsidy.

Sources: C. Beaton et al. 2013. *A Guide to Fossil Fuel Subsidy Reform for Policy-Makers in South East Asia.* Geneva: International Institute for Sustainable Development/Global Subsidies Initiative. https://www.iisd.org/gsi/sites/default/files/ffs_guidebook. pdf; GIZ. 2012. *International Fuel Prices 2010/2011.* Eschborn: Deutsche Gesellschaft für Internationale Zusammenarbeit; GIZ. 2015. *International Fuel Prices 2014.* Eschborn: Deutsche Gesellschaft für Internationale Zusammenarbeit.

A deeper understanding of the ways in which FFSs affect the wider economy, environment, and society requires the identification of subsidy beneficiaries and analysis of subsidy incidence. The incidence of a subsidy is the aspect of production or consumption it targets. This part of the analysis therefore seeks to identify to whom and for what a transfer is given. Subsidy incidence can refer to both producer and consumer subsidies. Examples of the former include measures that reduce the cost of labor, land, or natural resources. Two types of incidences relate to the direct consumption of fossil fuels and are common in DMCs: subsidies for the unit cost of consumption, which reduce the price paid by final consumers of fossil fuels, and subsidies that reduce the cost of energy purchases for households or enterprises at a rate that varies with income, such as lifeline tariffs for electricity (UNEP 2019). For detailed guidance, see Appendix, which shows the OECD matrix of support measures, broken down by transfer mechanism and subsidy incidence. DMC governments can use this matrix as a tool for analysis.

The aim of this step is to develop a clear understanding of the underlying mechanisms of fossil fuel support measures and their impacts, as well as the implications of FFSs for subsidy beneficiaries and for the wider economy, environment, and society. To examine the distribution of FFS benefits across income groups, DMC governments can draw on a wide range of tools. Publicly accessible tool kits for this purpose are provided by the Commitment to Equity Institute (CEQ Institute 2022) and the IMF.[9]

During analysis, policymakers should document the objectives of FFS and evaluate whether their rationales are still fulfilled or indeed desirable. The exercise is not straightforward, because those who are directly targeted and eligible for support through FFSs, whether industrial sectors or socially vulnerable groups, may not necessarily be those who ultimately benefit.

If the ultimate rationale of a specific subsidy remains in line with broader public policy goals such as protecting vulnerable social groups, DMC governments should design alternative measures and introduce appropriate institutional structures that can achieve the similar results without the negative climate, environmental, and health impacts of the FFS. If the subsidy has outlived its rationale, an alternative measure may not be required.

On the other hand, to minimize opposition and build consensus, some subsidy beneficiaries may need to be persuaded to support FFSR, notably powerful interest groups such as electricity generating companies and extractive industries. Addressing the concerns of these powerful groups may call for transitional mitigation measures. Whether they are necessary, and how they might be achieved, can be informed by the stakeholder mapping described in Box 24.

3. Map stakeholders and predict impacts from rationalization.

Price changes from FFSR will have numerous economic and social impacts. A good understanding of these impacts can reduce the risk of policy reversals.

Impacts from FFSR on households depend on a wide range of factors: the type of fuel subsidized, its importance in household budgets or for specific sectors, how much the fuel price affects prices for other goods and services, employment patterns, the structure of the economy, and subsidy beneficiaries.

For industry, impacts on international competitiveness depend on the energy intensity of traded sectors; developments in energy prices in competing countries; and the ability of businesses to respond through substitution, absorption, efficiency improvements, or price pass-through. In countries competing for the same markets, the immediate effect of energy price increases depends on how liberalized the energy market is in each country. If pass-through of international energy prices is similar across markets, impacts on production costs are also likely to be similar across countries (OECD 2010).

---

[9] For an introduction to the IMF tool for distributional incidence analysis and presentation of its methodology, see https://www.imf.org/external/pubs/ft/tnm/2016/tnm1607.pdf. An Excel template of the tool is available at https://www.imf.org/external/np/fad/subsidies/data/subsidiestemplate.xlsx.

Stakeholder Mapping, Consultation, and Engagement

When predicting impacts, it is necessary to identify key actors or stakeholders and understand and evaluate their concerns, to enable their inputs to inform fossil fuel subsidy rationalization from the outset. Stakeholder mapping is a relatively simple exercise whereby key stakeholders are listed and categorized, described in relation to key variables (e.g., interests, influence, resources, impacts, and importance), and mapped onto a matrix to facilitate easy comparison. Mapping can help pinpoint potential supporters and opponents of reform and deliver insights on stakeholder perspectives. It can also improve understanding of the complexity of stakeholder interests and concerns, which may change over time or in relation to different variables and inform strategies to obtain buy-in from various stakeholder groups.

If resources are limited, initial insights can be drawn from reviews of literature and media reports and interviews with business organizations and civil society. Ideally, reformers should hold public inquiries, run online and in-person consultations, create working groups with specific industrial sectors or other representative groups, and host workshops or road shows to facilitate exchange.

For more information, see especially Table 19 in Beaton et al. (2013).

Sources: C. Beaton et al. 2013. *A Guide to Fossil Fuel Subsidy Reform for Policy-Makers in South East Asia.* Geneva: International Institute for Sustainable Development/Global Subsidies Initiative. https://www.iisd.org/gsi/sites/default/files/ffs_guidebook.pdf; OECD. 2021. *OECD Companion to the Inventory of Support Measures for Fossil Fuels 2021.* Paris: Organisation for Economic Co-operation and Development. https://doi.org/10.1787/e670c620-en.

When assembling evidence, it is important to disaggregate data as much as possible. For example, understanding distributional impacts calls for analysis not only of household incomes but also of geographic disparities, household structures, and intersectional inequalities to ensure that overlapping dimensions of inequality are considered, such as disability, age, ethnicity, and gender.

Policymakers can draw on many qualitative approaches to predict the impacts of FFSR: checklists of common impacts, a literature review, historical analysis, conceptual mapping of fossil fuel use and impacts, identification of groups most reliant on fossil fuels, and scenario analysis. Throughout the entire process of preparing the ground and designing FFSR, stakeholders should be analyzed, consulted, and engaged (Box 24).

Policymakers can also use quantitative tools to understand FFSs and their impacts. This can include simple analysis using economic databases such as income and expenditure surveys, input–output tables, and social accounting matrixes. If resources are available, modeling tools may be useful to understand the fiscal, economic, environmental, and distributional impacts of FFSs and predict rationalization impacts. Microsimulation models using household and company surveys complement computable general equilibrium models and together can provide a fuller picture of reform impact over time on households, the economy, and GHG emissions, as well as predict behavioral responses to FFSR from producers and consumers. Modeling tools can be used to compare business as usual with one or more FFSR scenarios, indicating the broad trends to be anticipated, highlighting which stakeholders will be most affected, and suggesting how to allay their concerns.[10]

---

[10] Section 2 of OECD (2021) provides a very useful and detailed guide for using both quantitative and qualitative tools to inform FFSR design.

4. Draw up a priority list for rationalization.

Informed by the evidence base developed above, the final preparatory stage for DMC governments is to draw up a shortlist of possible measures for rationalization. This exercise should aim to rank subsidies in line with the gravity of their economic, social, and environmental impacts, while also taking political concerns into account. At this stage, governments should ascertain which impacts it is possible and feasible to mitigate, and which must be mitigated for political economy reasons to enable FFSR. Shortlisting should draw on the analysis conducted thus far and consider the following questions about the FFS:

(i)   Estimated cost: What is the burden of the subsidy on the budget?

(ii)   Distortion: How does it affect economic decision-making through prices, consumption, production, and investment?

(iii)   Environmental harm: How does it affect climate; biodiversity; and air, water, and soil quality?

(iv)   Social impacts: What are its health costs and implications for equity and welfare?

(v)   Effectiveness and subsidy incidence: Does the subsidy meet its objectives? Do intended beneficiaries actually benefit? Could the same objective be achieved in a way that is less environmentally harmful?

(vi)   Mitigation of impacts: Which impacts can and should be mitigated?

(vii) Political considerations: How may it be possible to build consensus and achieve political acceptance for rationalizing specific subsidies?

An effective and informative way to analyze the impacts of FFSs is to compare subsidies against a reference fiscal regime and/or other benchmarks, and to use discrepancies between the two to rank FFSs along different dimensions (OECD 2021, section 2.4). DMCs may also wish to compare possible mitigation measures along different dimensions—such as production, investment, consumption, environmental, and welfare implications—with a reference case without mitigation.

Governments will not be able to mitigate all impacts from price changes due to FFSR. Ultimately, they should not do so, as FFSR is intended to raise fossil fuel prices and engender behavioral responses to these higher prices. It is therefore necessary to prioritize impact mitigation, informed by several considerations: which stakeholders must be on side for reform to succeed, which vulnerable population groups must be protected for social justice reasons, and which specific mitigation measures can be implemented to build consensus.

Once alternative approaches to FFSR have been evaluated and ranked, the most feasible and desirable options should be taken forward for further consultation and potentially, to the strategic design stage. If particular FFSs cannot be rationalized at this time without serious economic or social disruption, or if mitigation is unlikely to be effective, other FFSs should be prioritized.

5. Strategic design of fossil fuel subsidy rationalization

Strategic design considerations do not follow a linear path in the same way as the preparatory stages above but may be undertaken simultaneously. Therefore, DMC governments may choose to develop a strategy for FFSR in which building institutions takes place in parallel with other elements of the design process or sequence their approach to strategic design in line with other political and regulatory developments. Nonetheless, all steps in the strategic design stage should ideally be completed to maximize the potential for rationalization to be successful in the longer term.

a. Institution Building

Depoliticize fossil fuel pricing. Regulating energy prices fosters a climate within which fossil fuel prices are highly politicized. Even in countries where energy prices are fully liberalized, FFSs influence the political discourse as beneficiaries seek to defend their interests whenever FFSR is discussed. Political opponents may exploit the powerful gravitational force that price controls and FFSs exert on politics when the political opportunity arises. As a result, rising prices and FFSR efforts tend to be met with political opposition and protest, sometimes achieving policy reversal. A key stage in the process of FFSR is thus often to take steps to visibly deny to governments the ability to manipulate fossil fuel prices for political ends. These kinds of considerations are particularly relevant in the case of energy price regulation—a common form of FFS in DMCs.

If fuel pricing mechanisms are retained, they should be made fully automatic, with decisions determined by an independent regulator without the involvement of politicians. In Ghana, for example, FFSR was supported by the newly created National Petroleum Authority—the board of which included government officials, representatives of trade unions and nongovernment organizations, and independent experts—to oversee an automatic fuel pricing mechanism and, later, deliver full fuel price liberalization.

If fuel pricing remains in the political domain, FFSR may not be sustained. This was the case in Nigeria in 2012, when a 117% increase in the gasoline price was met with nationwide protests and strikes. In response, the government scaled back the price increase to 49%, in effect retaining the subsidy at a lower level. DMCs may also choose to introduce a smoothing mechanism to mitigate global oil price fluctuations (Box 25).

Develop mechanisms to distribute targeted welfare. A survey of 32 developing countries in 2015 revealed that, on average, the wealthiest 20% of the population receives six times more in FFSs than the poorest 20%. This average masks disparities in benefits by type of subsidy: the wealthiest 20% of the population receives 27 times more in gasoline subsidies and 12 times more LPG subsidies (Coady, Flamini, and Sears 2015). Only kerosene subsidies benefit low-income households more and, even in this case, there is some subsidy leakage to higher-income groups.

FFS spending is substantial in several DMCs. In 2020, measured on the price gap approach, FFSs were worth $3.4 billion in Bangladesh, $16.0 billion in India, $9.9 billion in Kazakhstan, $3.5 billion in Malaysia, and $6.9 billion in Pakistan (IMF 2022). Unequal benefits from subsidies and their sheer size make a strong case for introducing targeted measures to support vulnerable households during FFSR and ensure that the burden of social assistance remains fiscally sustainable.

Box 25

Smoothing Mechanisms as an Option to Deal with International Price Volatility

To mitigate the risk of price shocks from international price volatility, governments may incorporate a smoothing rule in automatic pricing mechanisms. Limiting price increases to a maximum of 5% per month, for example, can avoid sharp increases in domestic prices, contain inflationary expectations, and dampen the effects of international price and exchange rate volatility. Smoothing should apply when prices rise or fall, to protect the budget over the medium term. A smoothing rule introduced in Peru in 2004 permits international prices to pass through to domestic markets if they are within a fixed price band, but if prices are below or above the band, they are absorbed by the general budget. In 2010, the band was updated to reflect trends in international prices. Regular review is important to ensure that stabilization funds are realistic and not at risk of exhausting their reserves at times of high international prices.

Sources: B. Clements et al., eds. 2013. *Energy Subsidy Reform: Lessons and Implications*. Washington, DC: International Monetary Fund. https://www.imf.org/en/Publications/Policy-Papers/Issues/2016/12/31/Energy-Subsidy-Reform-Lessons-and-Implications-PP4741; T. Laan, A. Suharsono, and B. Viswanathan. 2021. *Fuelling the Recovery: How India's Path from Fuel Subsidies to Taxes Can Help Indonesia*. Geneva: International Institute for Sustainable Development/Global Subsidies Initiative. https://www.iisd.org/system/files/2021-04/fuelling-recovery-india-subsidies-help-indonesia.pdf.

Like other forms of carbon pricing, an important benefit of FFSR is that it allows energy prices to rise and thus creates incentives for the more efficient fossil energy use. To retain this incentive, it is therefore desirable to design mitigation measures that do not reduce the price of energy but compensate the vulnerable in other ways, provided that welfare can be effectively targeted.

Figure 16 shows a hierarchy of types of measures that governments can consider. It uses a traffic light system: red for no action, amber for safeguarding measures, pale green for measures that generate additional benefits, and bright green for transformative measures.

Welfare can draw on and expand existing distributive mechanisms to safeguard vulnerable people. In Indonesia, for example, the operation of smart cards was expanded in 2015 to mitigate negative equity impacts due to FFSR.[11] Alternatively, social assistance can be realized through additional public services, preferably those that can be expanded quickly, such as eliminating fees for state schools, improving public transport, and increasing funding for health care, as was done in Ghana in 2014 (Whitley and van der Burg 2015). Finally, social assistance can be implemented through new programs that deliver co-benefits or even transformational change, such as benefits in kind, conditional cash transfers, or grants for renewable energy deployment. In India, grants covering 40% of the cost of rooftop solar panels are available for households, as is government support for farmers to install off-grid, solar-powered irrigation pumps (Garg et al. 2020).

---

[11] Indonesia's poverty reduction program is implemented using smart cards, which recipients of social assistance use to access food, cash transfers, health care, education, and other benefits. Cards are sent directly to households entitled to additional support (TNP2K, n.d.).

Figure 16: Hierarchy of Social Mitigation Measures

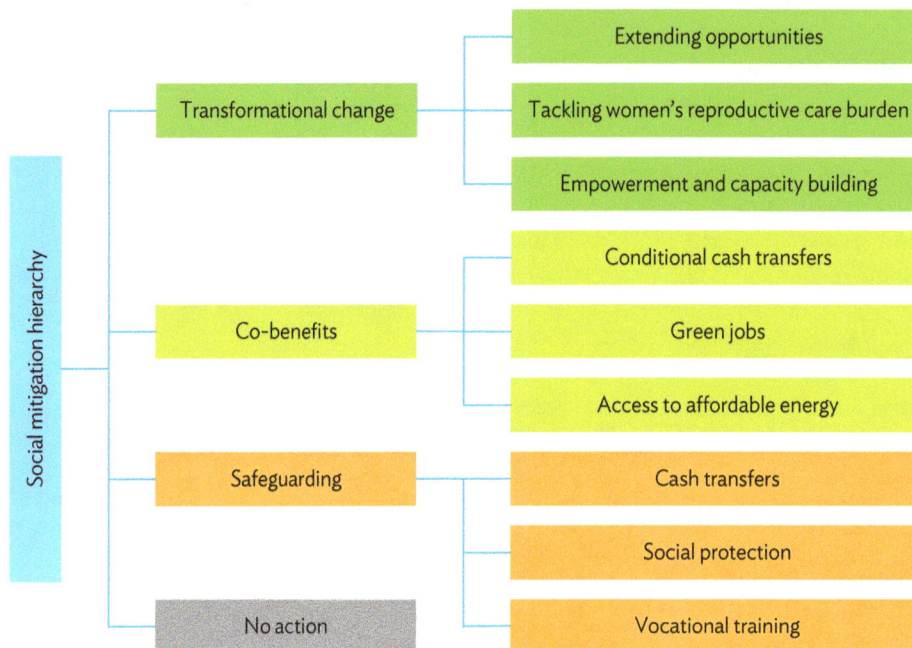

Source: K. Raworth, S. Wykes, and S. Bass. 2014. Securing Social Justice in Green Economies: A Review and Ten Considerations for Policymakers. *IIED Issue Paper*. London: International Institute for Environment and Development. https://pubs.iied.org/16578iied.

Design support for industry. If industry is likely to become less competitive, or if stakeholder consultations and mapping reveal a need to win support from key industries, support or mitigation measures that benefit industry may be required. Whatever the nature of these measures—direct support, tax expenditures, low-cost loans, grants, facilitated access to finance, or capacity building in the application of energy-efficient technologies—they should be targeted, temporary, time-limited, and subject to regular review to ensure that transitional support remains relevant and effective and does not become locked in and result in subsidy dependence.

A risk is that, if industries are entirely protected from the impact of FFSR, they will not innovate and adapt, thus undermining positive climate and environmental impacts. Measures should aim to mitigate short-term losses to ensure business continuity and enable substitutions, such as fuel-switching, and efficiency measures that reduce fossil fuel consumption. In this way, any support can ensure that industry builds resilience, improves energy efficiency, and reduces fossil fuel emissions. One of the least-distortive ways to protect competitiveness is to introduce FFSR gradually with sufficient lead-in time for affected firms to adopt mitigation measures. Much of the evidence for this "announcement effect" or "awareness effect" is anecdotal. However, in the United Kingdom, empirical research has shown that the announcement of the climate change levy—a downstream carbon-energy tax on industry— brought greater permanent reductions in energy demand than did the price effect of the levy alone (National Audit Office 2007).

Countries may also support firms' efforts to become more energy efficient or switch to renewable energy. In the Philippines, oil price deregulation and liberalization of the downstream oil industry took place in 1998 in parallel with the introduction of a National Energy Efficiency and Conservation Program, which aimed to increase the use of sustainable energy in homes, businesses, and transport. From 2000 to 2012, energy productivity improved by 75% (Nathan Associates 2016).

Solutions which target specific regions with high fossil fuel dependency within their economies can also be implemented. The rationalization of coal subsidies in Germany and Poland was accompanied by support for regional economic development, job creation, and social assistance to mitigate the impact of mining closures. These programs created new subsidies, but they focused resources on strengthening the local economy and social protection for affected workers.

Build capacity and consensus within the government. Designing FFSR requires cooperation across government—including ministries responsible for fiscal policy, energy, finance, economy, industry, planning, investment, labor and social issues, the environment, and climate—to ensure that all relevant factors are taken into consideration. An integrated approach can be fostered by creating a high-level committee to make decisions and an interministerial working group at the operative level.

In DMCs where FFSs are a form of untargeted social assistance, rationalization is a structural process that will deliver a more efficient and greener economy and a more sophisticated and targeted welfare state. To achieve this transition, capacity building for ministry staff is indispensable to increase awareness and knowledge of how to analyze modeling findings; design automatic pricing mechanisms; and design, administer, and effectively target social welfare. DMCs can request support from international development agencies and development banks, including ADB, to realize this process. Capacity building can also have the additional benefit of making the government more politically credible in the eyes of key stakeholders. This matters because a government that is poorly administered or ineffective in delivering services has little to offer special interest groups opposed to FFSR.

There is an international consensus that FFSs should be rationalized. DMC governments typically have to work hard to translate this consensus into national terms, yet it is important that they do so. Strong leadership and government cohesion are key success factors for FFSR. Lead ministers and ministries seeking to initiate FFSR must strive to build consensus across government, working with and bringing on board all relevant ministries and agencies. Creating high-level interministerial committees and working groups cultivates a whole-of-government approach to the design and implementation of a rationalization strategy, enabling effective political decisions to be made and appropriate operational steps to be taken.

Interministerial groups can be supplemented with cross-party parliamentary groups, or advisory groups of independent experts, such as green fiscal commissions. In Malaysia, a policy lab approach is often used to solve difficult political problems, with the 2010 subsidy rationalization lab bringing together 70 experts who worked with the cabinet to develop a detailed FFSR plan. An open day was subsequently held to publish results and collate feedback. Findings ultimately fed into subsidy rationalization recommendations for the Prime Minister (Beaton et al. 2013). Nonetheless, it took time before the reform of subsidies for gasoline and diesel was finally initiated in September 2013 (Bridel and Lontoh 2014).

b. Time Frame

Pacing and timing. Experience suggests that, as a rule, gradual FFSR tends to be more sustainable than a "big bang" approach, though, in some circumstances, governments may have no alternative to rapid reform—if, for example, budgetary pressures are ruinous. In general, if prices for consumers are well below global prices, it is difficult to transition to full pass-through of international fossil energy prices in one step without risking a political crisis. Incremental approaches to FFSR allow time for consultation and the implementation of complementary measures to prevent negative distributive and competitiveness impacts, and to facilitate the communication of a clear timeline.

Strategic timing may be another critical success factor. Implementing reform while seasonal fossil fuel consumption is low may reduce opposition and give consumers time to adjust to higher prices. Implementing FFSR during periods of low inflation can dampen inflation shocks (Box 26). Timing FFSR to coincide with a broader process of fiscal reform may reduce opposition to FFSR elements and free up revenue for the introduction of social assistance programs.

Box 26

Inflation and Fossil Fuel Subsidy Rationalization

Increased energy prices have short-term impacts on inflation, which may give rise to expectations of price and wage increases over the longer term. The extent to which higher energy costs cause inflation and persistently higher prices depends on the strength of second-round effects of inflation on wages and prices for other inputs. Policymakers may be able to contain these effects with appropriate monetary and fiscal policies, including efforts to enhance domestic revenue mobilization and improve targeted social assistance packages. Fossil fuel subsidy rationalization helps support an appropriate fiscal policy response to inflation by reducing budget deficits and helping to contain demand pressure on prices. A report prepared by the International Monetary Fund (2011) is a useful guide to possible monetary and fiscal policy responses to inflation shocks, with a particular focus on low-income countries.

Sources: International Monetary Fund. 2011. *Managing Global Growth Risks and Commodity Price Shocks—Vulnerabilities and Policy Challenges for Low-Income Countries*. Washington, DC. https://www.imf.org/external/np/pp/eng/2011/092111. pdf; B. Clements et al., eds. 2013. *Energy Subsidy Reform: Lessons and Implications*. Washington, DC: International Monetary Fund. https://www.imf.org/en/Publications/Policy-Papers/Issues/2016/12/31/Energy-Subsidy-Reform-Lessons-and-Implications-PP4741.

An opportunity to rationalize FFSs may arise in a crisis and a government's response to it. Crises often radically boost the credibility of reformers and, in some cases, there may simply be no other alternative available to governments. In the Dominican Republic in 2012, corruption scandals linked to the head of the electricity company sparked street protests and made clear the political cost of not reforming the energy system (Inchauste and Victor 2017). In the coming years, some countries may have little alternative but to withdraw price regulations and allow international energy price volatility to pass through to energy consumers.

Anticipating falls in international oil and gas prices can create windows of opportunity for FFSR. Under such conditions, even relatively significant fuel price increases do not necessarily raise the domestic fuel price above a high global price. From 2015 to 2017, countries around the world, including Indonesia, India, and Malaysia, took advantage of low oil and gas prices to phase out consumer FFSs.

Sequencing subsidy rationalization. The objective of sequencing is to prevent policy reversals by carefully selecting which FFSs to rationalize first. Concerns about distributional impacts cause many countries to rationalize first subsidies for goods or services largely consumed by wealthier households. This approach leaves time for policymakers to learn and to test the effectiveness of complementary support measures, while minimizing negative distributional impacts.

If taking this approach, policymakers should bear in mind that retaining untargeted subsidies over the longer term is inefficient and may prove costly, not least because such expenditure is vulnerable to fluctuations in global prices for fossil fuels. It is therefore desirable that price subsidies for goods consumed by lower-income groups, notably kerosene and LPG, are rationalized as soon as politically feasible, and that targeted and effective social assistance programs be established to expedite this.

Theoretically, the most economically and fiscally efficient approach to carbon pricing is for policymakers to rationalize all FFSs, i.e., to correct all negative carbon prices, and only then introduce carbon pricing through taxes and emission trading. In practice, most countries see some overlap between FFSR and the introduction of carbon pricing. Many OECD countries have reformed the most explicit and easily identifiable FFSs and introduced carbon pricing. Yet, subsidies remain for both producers and consumers, as OECD inventories of FFS measures show. These rather muddled outcomes are likely to be emulated in DMCs.

Sequencing FFSR has drawbacks. Budgetary savings are lower, and sequencing can distort consumption patterns, incentivizing fuel adulteration, smuggling, and the redirection of cheaper fuels to transportation. In Türkiye, for example, LPG subsidies were phased out more rapidly than initially envisaged in response to a sharp increase in consumption and LPG conversion in vehicles (Clements et al. 2013). A slower process may allow time for opposition to FFSR to coalesce. Ultimately, a strategic approach to the FFSR time frame is essential, whether gradual or rapid (Box 27).

c. Communication and Consensus Building

Engaging stakeholders within and beyond government is critical for successful FFSR implementation. Early consultation can help governments understand stakeholder perspectives and identify FFSR winners and losers. Engagement also enables the valid concerns of stakeholders to feed into FFSR design and mitigation measures.

Later in the process, stakeholder consultation can build consensus and facilitate the collaborative development of politically acceptable solutions and may also provide insights on external perceptions and misperceptions of the government and FFSR. Engaging stakeholders cultivates transparency and creates ownership and a sense of empowerment, which may help secure buy-in and build consensus in favor of FFSR.

> **Box 27**
>
> ## Big Bang in Iran: Strategic Pacing, Timing, and Sequencing
>
> Fossil fuel subsidy rationalization in Iran in 2010 was very carefully designed, with strategic pacing, timing, and sequencing able to foster widespread support. Fossil fuel subsidies for consumers were reformed in December, when energy consumption tends to be lowest. Bank accounts were opened for some 80% of citizens, and cash transfers were deposited into these accounts from October 2010, 2 months before subsidy rationalization. When price ceilings were lifted in December 2010, beneficiaries were granted access to their accounts. This strategy facilitated a big bang approach. In the first year, fossil fuel subsidies worth $50 billion–$60 billion were cut. The public received $30 billion in transfers, and the poverty rate declined from 23% to 11%. Industry received $10 billion–$15 billion for restructuring to reduce energy intensity.
>
> The Iran case demonstrates the clear advantage of a big bang approach: It can facilitate radical decision-making within government, such as the introduction of a universal cash transfer to citizens. However, it also exemplifies the importance of developing administrative systems to target welfare to the poorest households, to ensure that combating poverty is affordable in the long term. In Iran, inflation has eroded the real value of compensation payments such that over time, the poorest households lost half of the initial benefit from cash transfers. Attempts to target cash transfers to lower-income deciles have not been particularly successful.
>
> Sources: D. Guillaume, R. Zytek, and M. R. Farzin. 2011. Iran: The Chronicles of the Subsidy Reform. *IMF Working Paper*. 11/167. Washington, DC: International Monetary Fund; A. Enami and N. Lustig. 2018. Inflation and the Erosion of the Poverty Reduction Impact of Iran's Universal Cash Transfer. *CEQ Working Paper*. 68. New Orleans: Commitment to Equity Institute. http://repec.tulane.edu/RePEc/ceq/ceq68.pdf.

A key stakeholder in any FFSR is the citizenry of the country, whose support or lack of it can prove decisive. Because the public tends to know little about energy pricing—or about the unequal distribution of subsidy benefits, negative effects of FFSs, or potential gains from FFSR—building public consensus generally calls for a well-designed and targeted public information campaign. A communication strategy can combat information deficits and, by highlighting the benefits and advantages of FFSR, help to build consensus in favor of reform.

The groundwork for FFSR should provide the evidence and analysis necessary to develop a targeted strategic communications campaign. An idealized model of campaign development is shown in Figure 17. Drawing on the results of stakeholder mapping to define the audience, the development of audience-specific messaging and the selection of appropriate media approaches is essential to ensure that communication is relevant, effective, and able to speak to various audiences in a way that can engage them and address their concerns.

Campaign objectives should be clearly defined from the outset and may include

(i)   raising awareness of the negative impacts of FFSs and the benefits of rationalization,

(ii)   improving budgetary transparency,

(iii)   building support for change by publicizing the reallocation of revenue or other measures, and

(iv)   informing key stakeholders about FFSR strategies and mitigation measures.

Figure 17: Idealized Model of Communication Campaign Development

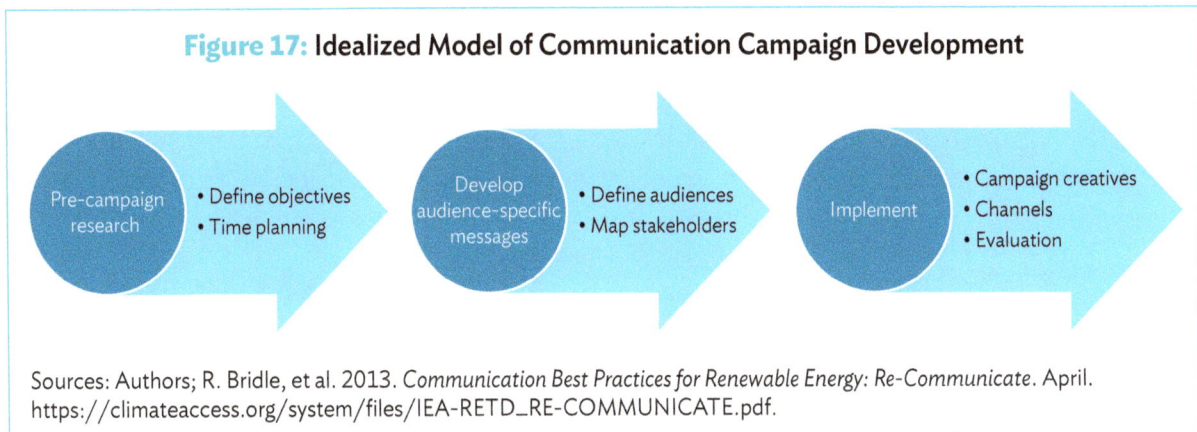

Sources: Authors; R. Bridle, et al. 2013. *Communication Best Practices for Renewable Energy: Re-Communicate*. April. https://climateaccess.org/system/files/IEA-RETD_RE-COMMUNICATE.pdf.

Others can be brought onside by involving in communication campaigns the firms or interest groups that benefit from and therefore support FFSR. Depending on the country and target audience, DMCs may use—individually or in any combination—news media, social media, television, cinema advertisements, billboards, leaflets, flyers, and citizens' guides. The Global Subsidy Initiative has developed a number of citizens' guides, including for Malaysia (GSI 2013) and Indonesia (GSI, n.d.).

Communicating positive outcomes and drawing on successes can inform subsequent rounds of FFSR. Indonesia's voluntary self-report in the Group of Twenty peer review process examines the country's efforts to rationalize FFSs and looks to the future, drawing on previous experience to delineate possible next steps, including electricity subsidy reform and efforts to reduce electricity prices over the long term by encouraging renewable energy investment through tax incentives, and redirecting financing streams on the basis of information attained through climate budget tagging.[12]

6. Monitoring and adjustment

Predicting the impacts of FFSR is not a simple exercise, and changes in any number of factors may have unexpected effects. Monitoring impacts during the rationalization process is therefore essential to identify and rectify any unexpected outcomes such as smuggling, unwanted fuel substitutions, poor operation of social mitigation policies, unpredicted impacts on vulnerable social groups, or negative impacts on certain industries.

Governments may need to adjust compensation measures and expand their coverage or improve the administration of support mechanisms for business. In the longer term, adjustments may need to be made to ensure that policies remain relevant, and that the positive benefits of social assistance are not undermined. In Iran, high inflation eroded the real value of cash transfers by half from 2011 to 2016, with rural areas particularly hard hit (Enami and Lustig 2018). Policy reviews and lessons learned throughout the process can inform the next round of FFSR.

---

[12] This tagging approach alerts the government on the volume of climate financing across several line ministries and highlights where finance is lacking and has thus informed an increase in climate change financing (MEMR and MOF 2019).

C. Concluding Words

FFSR is challenging and politically sensitive. Subsidies are deeply embedded in the economies and fiscal systems of many countries. Without high investment in renewable energy and strong political commitment to energy transition and green economy transformation—and political will to make FFSR an integral part of this transformation—subsidies are unlikely to be rationalized, especially the more hidden subsidies.[13]

Yet, disentangling the subsidy knot is a challenge to which governments all over the world must respond to meet the targets of the Paris Agreement. To make good on their NDCs, DMCs need to explore which options for carbon pricing are likely to prove effective, workable, and politically feasible. FFSR and other carbon pricing approaches will be necessary for DMCs to deliver on their NDCs and achieve the Sustainable Development Goals of Agenda 2030 effectively and efficiently. Based on the political context in their country, some DMCs may choose to introduce carbon pricing and taxation, as described in Chapters 2 and 3 of this report, even before the process of rationalization is complete.

---

[13]   See Cottrell, Fortier, and Schlegelmilch (2015) for a detailed analysis of the interactions between FFSR and renewable energy transition, and the ways in which transition to renewable energy can facilitate reform.

OECD MATRIX OF SUPPORT MEASURES, WITH EXAMPLES

TRANSFER MECHANISM (how a transfer is created)	STATUTORY OR FORMAL INCIDENCE (to whom and for what a transfer is given)								
	Production				Cost of production factors			Direct consumption	
	Output returns	Enterprise income	Cost of intermediate inputs	Labor	Land	Capital	Knowledge	Unit cost of consumption	Household or enterprise income
Direct transfer of funds	Output bounty or deficiency payment	Operating grant	Input-price subsidy	Wage subsidy	Capital grant linked to acquisition of land	Capital grant linked to capital	Government R&D	Unit subsidy	Government-subsidized lifeline electricity rate
Tax revenue foregone	Production tax credit	Reduced rate of income tax	Reduction in excise tax on output	Reduction in social charges (payroll taxes)	Property tax reduction or exemption	Investment tax credit	Tax credit for private R&D	VAT or excise tax concession on fuel	Tax deduction related to energy purchases that exceed given share of income
Other government revenue foregone			Underpricing of a government good or service		Underpricing of access to government land or natural resources; reduction of resource royalty or extraction tax		Government transfer of intellectual property right (IPR)	Underpricing of access to a natural resource harvested by final consumer	
Transfer of risk to government	Government buffer stock	Third-party liability limit for producers	Provision of security (e.g., military protection of supply lines)	Assumption of occupational health and accident liabilities	Credit guarantee linked to acquisition of land	Credit guarantee linked to capital		Price-triggered subsidy	Means-tested cold-weather grant
Induced transfers	Import tariff or export subsidy	Monopoly concession	Monopsony concession; export restriction	Wage control	Land-use control	Credit control (sector-specific)	Deviations from standard IPR rules	Regulated price; cross-subsidy	Mandated lifeline electricity rate

IPR = intellectual property rights, OECD = Organisation for Economic Co-operation and Development, R&D = research and development, VAT = value-added tax.

Source: OECD. 2013. Analysing Energy Subsidies in the Countries of Eastern Europe, Caucasus and Central Asia. Paris: Organisation for Economic Co-operation and Development. https://www.oecd.org/env/outreach/energy_subsidies.pdf.

REFERENCES

Adolf, C. et al. 2014. TTIP and Fossil Fuel Subsidies: Using International Policy Processes as Entry Points for Reform in the EU and the USA. *Heinrich Boell Stiftung TTIP Series.* https://eu.boell.org/sites/default/files/hbs_ttip_fossil_fuel_subsidies_1.pdf.

Alonso, C. and J. Kilpatrick. 2022. The Distributional Impact of a Carbon Tax in Asia and the Pacific. *IMF Working Paper.* 116. Washington, DC: International Monetary Fund.

Andersen, M. S. 2010. Europe's Experience with Carbon-Energy Taxation. *Sapiens.* 3(2). http://sapiens.revues.org/index1072.html.

Andersen M. S. and P. Ekins. 2009. *Carbon-Energy Taxation: Lessons from Europe.* New York: Oxford University Press. https://doi.org/10.1093/acprof:oso/9780199570683.001.0001.

Asian Development Bank (ADB). 2016a. *Emissions Trading Schemes and Their Linking: Challenges and Opportunities in Asia and the Pacific.* Manila. https://www.adb.org/sites/default/files/publication/182501/emissions-trading-schemes.pdf.

———. 2016b. *Fossil Fuel Subsidies in Asia: Trends, Impacts, and Reforms: Integrative Report.* Manila. https://www.adb.org/publications/fossil-fuel-subsidies-asia-trends-impacts-and-reforms.

———. 2019. *Article 6 of the Paris Agreement: Drawing Lessons from the Joint Crediting Mechanism.* Manila. https://dx.doi.org/10.22617/TIM190555-2.

Barker, T. et al. 2009. The Effects of Environmental Tax Reform on International Competitiveness in the European Union: Modelling with E3ME. In M. S. Anderson and P. Ekins, eds. *Carbon-Energy Taxation: Lessons from Europe.* New York: Oxford University Press. pp. 147–214. https://doi.org/10.1093/acprof:oso/9780199570683.001.0001.

Baron, R. 2012. *Setting Caps: Partnership for Market Readiness Technical Workshop: Domestic Emissions Trading.* Paris: International Energy Agency. https://www.thepmr.org/system/files/documents/Cap%20Seting%20in%20Emissions%20Trading%20-%20Expert%20View.pdf.

Beaton, C. et al. 2013. *A Guide to Fossil Fuel Subsidy Reform for Policy-Makers in South East Asia.* Geneva: International Institute for Sustainable Development/Global Subsidies Initiative. https://www.iisd.org/gsi/sites/default/files/ffs_guidebook.pdf.

Beaton, C., L. Lontoh, and M. Wai-Poi. 2017. Indonesia: Pricing Reforms, Social Assistance, and the Importance of Perceptions. In G. Inchauste and D. G. Victor, eds. *The Political Economy of Energy Subsidy Reform.* Directions in Development. Washington, DC: World Bank. https://openknowledge.worldbank.org/bitstream/handle/10986/26216/9781464810077.pdf.

Bird, N. et al. 2013. *Using a Life Cycle Assessment Approach to Estimate the Net Greenhouse Gas Emissions of Bioenergy.* IEA Bioenergy. https://www.ieabioenergy.com/wp-content/uploads/2013/10/Using-a-LCA-approach-to-estimate-the-net-GHG-emissions-of-bioenergy.pdf.

Breuing, J. 2020. *A Revision of Ukraine's Carbon Tax*. Berlin: Berlin Economics. https://www.lowcarbonukraine.com/wp-content/uploads/A-Revision-of-Ukraines-Carbon-Tax.pdf.

Bridel, A. and L. Lontoh. 2014. *Lessons Learned: Malaysia's 2013 Subsidy Reform*. Geneva: International Institute for Sustainable Development. https://www.iisd.org/gsi/sites/default/files/ffs_malaysia_lessonslearned.pdf.

Bridle, R. et al. 2013. *Communication Best Practices for Renewable Energy: Re-Communicate*. April. https://foes.de/pdf/2013-04-IEA-RETD-RE-COMMUNICATE-Report.pdf.

Carbon Market Institute. *COP26 Key Takeaways: Article 6 Explainer*. https://carbonmarketinstitute.org/app/uploads/2021/11/COP26-Glasgow-Article-6-Explainer.pdf.

Cekindo. 2022. *The Important Things to Know about Indonesia's Carbon Tax*. https://www.cekindo.com/blog/indonesia-carbon-tax.

Center for Climate and Energy Solutions. *Carbon Border Adjustments*. https://www.c2es.org/content/carbon-border-adjustments/.

CEQ Institute. 2022. *CEQ Handbook: Estimating the Impact of Fiscal Policy on Inequality and Poverty*. https://commitmentoequity.org/publications-ceq-handbook.

Chantanusornsiri, W. 2021. Excise Considers Carbon Tax. *Bangkok Post*. 4 October. https://www.bangkokpost.com/business/2191891/excise-considers-carbon-tax.

Clements, B. et al., eds. 2013. *Energy Subsidy Reform: Lessons and Implications*. Washington, DC: International Monetary Fund. https://www.imf.org/en/Publications/Policy-Papers/Issues/2016/12/31/Energy-Subsidy-Reform-Lessons-and-Implications-PP4741.

ClimateWorks Foundation. 2010. Australian Carbon Trust Report: Commercial Buildings Emissions Reduction Opportunities. December. https://www.climateworkscentre.org/wp-content/uploads/2019/10/climateworks_commercial_buildings_emission_reduction_opportunities_dec2010.pdf (accessed 1 June 2023).

Coady, D., V. Flamini, and L. Sears. 2015. The Unequal Benefits of Fuel Subsidies Revisited: Evidence for Developing Countries. *IMF Working Paper* 15/250. Washington, DC: International Monetary Fund. https://doi.org/10.5089/9781513501390.001.

Coady, D. et al. 2019. *Global Fossil Fuel Subsidies Remain Large: An Update Based on Country-Level Estimates. IMF Working Paper*. 19/89. Washington, DC: International Monetary Fund.

Cottrell, J. 2014. Reforming EHS in Europe: Success Stories, Failures and Agenda-Setting. In F. Oosterhuis and P. ten Brink, eds. *Paying the Polluter: Environmentally Harmful Subsidies and Their Reform*. Cheltenham: Edward Elgar.

Cottrell, J., F. Fortier, and K. Schlegelmilch. 2015. *Fossil Fuel to Renewable Energy: Comparator Study of Subsidy Reforms and Energy Transitions in African and Indian Ocean Island States*. Incheon: United Nations Office for Sustainable Development. https://www.lerenovaveis.org/contents/lerpublication/UNOSD_2015_JAN_Fossil_Fuel_to_Renewable_Energy.pdf.

Couharde, C. and S. Mouhoud. 2018. Fossil Fuel Subsidies, Income Inequality and Poverty: Evidence from Developing Countries. *Working Paper*. 2018-42. Paris: Economix. https://economix.fr/pdf/dt/2018/WP_EcoX_2018-42.pdf.

Crippa, M. et al. 2021. *Fossil CO_2 Emissions of All World Countries*. Ispra, Italy: Joint Research Centre. https://publications.jrc.ec.europa.eu/repository/handle/JRC121460.

Danish Energy Agency. 2014. Danish carbon emissions continue to drop. Press release. 12 May. https://ens.dk/en/press/danish-carbon-emissions-continue-drop (accessed 1 June 2023).

Datta, A. 2010. The Incidence of Fuel Taxation in India. *Energy Economics*. 32. pp. S26–S33. https://doi.org/10.1016/j.eneco.2009.10.007.

Deloitte. *What the New Carbon Tax Means for SA Industry*. https://www2.deloitte.com/za/en/pages/tax/articles/what-the-new-carbon-tax-means-for-SA-industry.html.

Di Maria, C., M. Zarkovic, and B. Hintermann. 2020. Are Emissions Trading Schemes Cost-effective? *Working Paper*. 2020/13. Faculty of Business and Economics, University of Basel. https://ideas.repec.org/p/bsl/wpaper/2020-13.html.

Dorband, I. I. et al. 2019. Poverty and Distributional Effects of Carbon Pricing in Low- and Middle-Income Countries: A Global Comparative Analysis. *World Development*. 115. pp. 246–257. https://doi.org/10.1016/j.worlddev.2018.11.015.

Dufrasne, G. 2021. *FAQ: Deciphering Article 6 of the Paris Agreement*. Carbon Market Watch. https://carbonmarketwatch.org/2021/12/10/faq-deciphering-article-6-of-the-paris-agreement/.

Dussaux, D. 2019. The Joint Effects of Energy Prices and Carbon Taxes on Environmental and Economic Performance: Evidence from the French Manufacturing Sector. *OECD Environment Working Paper*. 154. Paris: Organisation for Economic Co-operation and Development. https://dx.doi.org/10.1787/b84b1b7d-en.

Eden, A. et al. 2018. *Benefits of Emissions Trading: Taking Stock of the Impacts of Emissions Trading Systems Worldwide*. Berlin: International Carbon Action Partnership. https://icapcarbonaction.com/system/files/document/benefits-of-ets_updated-august-2018.pdf.

Enami, A. and N. Lustig. 2018. Inflation and the Erosion of the Poverty Reduction Impact of Iran's Universal Cash Transfer. *CEQ Working Paper*. 68. New Orleans: Commitment to Equity Institute. http://repec.tulane.edu/RePEc/ceq/ceq68.pdf.

EUR-Lex. *Commission Implementing Regulation (EU) 2018/2066 of 19 December 2018 on the Monitoring and Reporting of Greenhouse Gas Emissions Pursuant to Directive 2003/87/EC of the European Parliament and of the Council and Amending Commission Regulation (EU) No. 601/2012 (Text with EEA Relevance)*. https://eur-lex.europa.eu/legal-content/en/TXT/?uri=CELEX%3A32018R2066.

————. 2003. *Article 17.1a of Council Directive 2003/96/EC Restructuring the Community Framework for the Taxation of Energy Products and Electricity*. https://eur-lex.europa.eu/legal-content/EN/TXT/?uri=celex%3A32003L0096.

———. 2021. *Proposal for a Regulation of the European Parliament and of the Council Establishing a Carbon Border Adjustment Mechanism, COM(2021)564 final*. https://eur-lex.europa.eu/legal-content/EN/TXT/?uri=celex:52021PC0564.

European Commission. 2015. *EU ETS Handbook*. https://ec.europa.eu/clima/system/files/2017-03/ets_handbook_en.pdf.

———. 2021. *Questions and Answers—Emissions Trading—Putting a Price on Carbon*. https://ec.europa.eu/commission/presscorner/detail/en/qanda_21_3542.

Feng, K. et al. 2018. Managing the Distributional Effects of Energy Taxes and Subsidy Removal in Latin America and the Caribbean. *Applied Energy*. 225. pp. 424–436. https://doi.org/10.1016/j.apenergy.2018.04.116.

Fitz Gerald, J. et al. 2009. Assessing Vulnerability of Selected Sectors under Environmental Tax Reform. In M. S. Andersen and P. Ekins, eds. *Carbon-Energy Taxation: Lessons from Europe*. New York: Oxford University Press. pp. 55–76. https://doi.org/10.1093/acprof:oso/9780199570683.001.0001.

Fonseca-Gómez, M. 2018. *Colombia Introduces Carbon Tax*. Environment for Development Initiative. https://www.efdinitiative.org/sites/default/files/publications/colombia_final.pdf.

Frey, M. 2017. Assessing the Impact of a Carbon Tax in Ukraine. *Climate Policy*. 17(3). pp. 378–396. https://doi.org/10.1080/14693062.2015.1096230.

G20. 2009. *Leaders' Statement: The Pittsburgh Summit*. Pittsburgh: Group of Twenty. http://www.g20.utoronto.ca/2009/2009communique0925.html.

Garg, V. et al. 2020. *Mapping India's Energy Subsidies 2020: Fossil Fuels, Renewables, and Electric Vehicles*. Geneva: International Institute for Sustainable Development. https://www.iisd.org/publications/report/mapping-indias-energy-subsidies-2020-fossil-fuels-renewables-and-electric.

GIZ. 2012. *International Fuel Prices 2010/2011*. Eschborn: Deutsche Gesellschaft für Internationale Zusammenarbeit.

———. 2015. *International Fuel Prices 2014*. Eschborn: Deutsche Gesellschaft für Internationale Zusammenarbeit.

Goulder, L. 1995. Environmental Taxation and the "Double Dividend": A Reader's Guide. *International Tax and Public Finance*. 2(2). pp. 157–183. https://link.springer.com/article/10.1007/BF00877495.

Greenhouse Gas Management Institute and Stockholm Environment Institute. *Carbon Offset Projects*. https://www.offsetguide.org/understanding-carbon-offsets/carbon-offset-projects/.

GSI. *Panduan Masyarakat Tentang Subsidi Energi di Indonesia*. Geneva: International Institute for Sustainable Development/Global Subsidies Initiative. https://www.iisd.org/system/files/publications/indonesia_czguide_ind.pdf.

———. 2013. *A Citizens' Guide to Energy Subsidies in Malaysia*. Geneva: International Institute for Sustainable Development/Global Subsidies Initiative. https://www.iisd.org/gsi/sites/default/files/ffs_malaysia_czguide.pdf.

Guillaume, D., R. Zytek, and M. R. Farzin. 2011. Iran: The Chronicles of the Subsidy Reform. *IMF Working Paper*. 11/167. Washington, DC: International Monetary Fund.

Haites, E. 2018. Carbon Taxes and Greenhouse Gas Emissions Trading Systems: What Have We Learned? *Climate Policy*. 18(8). pp. 955–966. https://doi.org/10.1080/14693062.2018.1492897.

Healy, S. 2018. *Setting the ETS Cap: Options for a Mexican ETS*. Öko-Institut. https://iki-alliance.mx/wp-content/uploads/4.-ETS-Cap-Setting_Oeko-Institut.pdf.

High-Level Commission on Carbon Prices. 2017. Report of the High-Level Commission on Carbon Prices. Washington, DC: World Bank. https://static1.squarespace.com/static/54ff9c5ce4b0a53decccfb4c/t/59b7f2409f8dce5316811916/1505227332748/CarbonPricing_FullReport.pdf.

Inchauste, G. and D. G. Victor, eds. 2017. *The Political Economy of Energy Subsidy Reform. Directions in Development*. Washington, DC: World Bank. https://openknowledge.worldbank.org/bitstream/handle/10986/26216/9781464810077.pdf.

International Carbon Action Partnership (ICAP). *Allocation*. Berlin: International Carbon Action Partnership. https://icapcarbonaction.com/en/allocation.

—————. 2021. ICAP ETS Briefs. Berlin: International Carbon Action Partnership. https://icapcarbonaction.com/en/publications/icap-ets-briefs.

—————. 2022a. *Emissions Trading Worldwide: Status Report 2022*. Berlin: International Carbon Action Partnership. https://icapcarbonaction.com/system/files/document/220408_icap_report_exsum_en.pdf.

—————. 2022b. *Indonesia* [factsheet]. Berlin: International Carbon Action Partnership. https://icapcarbonaction.com/system/files/ets_pdfs/icap-etsmap-factsheet-104.pdf.

International Energy Agency (IEA). *Defining the Role*. Paris: International Energy Agency. https://www.iea.org/reports/implementing-effective-emissions-trading-systems/defining-the-role.

—————. 1999. The World Energy Outlook. Looking at Energy Subsidies: Getting the Prices Right. Paris: International Energy Agency. https://doi.org/10.1787/weo-1999-en.

—————. 2020. *Implementing Effective Emissions Trading Systems: Lessons from International Experiences*. Paris: OECD Publishing. https://doi.org/10.1787/b7d0842b-en.

—————. 2022. *Energy Subsidies: Tracking the Impact of Fossil-Fuel Subsidies*. Paris: International Energy Agency.

International Monetary Fund (IMF). 2011. *Managing Global Growth Risks and Commodity Price Shocks —Vulnerabilities and Policy Challenges for Low-Income Countries*. Washington, DC: IMF. https://www.imf.org/external/np/pp/eng/2011/092111.pdf.

—————. 2022. *Climate Change: Fossil Fuel Subsidies*. Washington, DC: International Monetary Fund. https://www.imf.org/en/Topics/climate-change/energy-subsidies.

IMF and OECD. 2021. *Tax Policy and Climate Change: IMF/OECD Report for the G20*. https://www.oecd.org/tax/tax-policy/imf-oecd-g20-report-tax-policy-and-climate-change.htm.

Interpol Environmental Crimes Programme. 2013. *Guide to Carbon Trading Crime.* Lyon: Interpol. https://www.interpol.int/content/download/5172/file/Guide%20to%20Carbon%20Trading%20Crime.pdf.

Jaeger, W. K. 2012. The Double Dividend Debate. In J. Milne and M. S. Andersen, eds. *Handbook of Research on Environmental Taxation.* Cheltenham: Edward Elgar. pp. 211–229. https://doi.org/10.4337/9781781952146.00021.

Keseljevic, A. and M. Koman. 2015. Analysis of the Effects of Introduction of an Additional Carbon Tax on the Slovenian Economy Considering Different Forms of Recycling. *Economic and Business Review.* 16(3). pp. 247–277. https://www.ebrjournal.net/home/vol16/iss3/.

Knoema.com. 2021. International Carbon Tax: Who Will Pay for the EU's Green Future? Blog. https://knoema.com/infographics/pgtukpc/international-carbon-tax-who-will-pay-for-the-eu-s-green-future.

Koh, J. et al. 2021. Impacts of Carbon Pricing on Developing Economies. *International Journal of Energy Economics and Policy.* 11(4). pp. 298–311. https://doi.org/10.32479/ijeep.11201.

Kumenov, A. and J. Lillis. 2022. Kazakhstan Explainer: Why Did Fuel Prices Spike, Bringing Protesters Out onto the Streets? *Eurasianet.* 4 January. https://eurasianet.org/kazakhstan-explainer-why-did-fuel-prices-spike-bringing-protesters-out-onto-the-streets.

Laan, T., A. Suharsono, and B. Viswanathan. 2021. *Fuelling the Recovery: How India's Path from Fuel Subsidies to Taxes Can Help Indonesia.* Geneva: International Institute for Sustainable Development/Global Subsidies Initiative. https://www.iisd.org/system/files/2021-04/fuelling-recovery-india-subsidies-help-indonesia.pdf.

Lenain, P. 2022. Denmark's Green Tax Reform: G20 Countries Should Take Notice. Council on Economic Policies. https://www.cepweb.org/denmarks-green-tax-reform-g20-countries-should-take-notice/ (accessed 1 June 2023).

MEMR and MOF. 2019. *Indonesia's Efforts to Phase Out and Rationalise Its Fossil Fuel Subsidies. A Self-Report on the G20 Peer Review of Inefficient Fossil Fuel Subsidies that Encourage Wasteful Consumption in Indonesia.* Jakarta: Ministry of Energy and Mineral Resources and Ministry of Finance, Government of Indonesia. https://www.oecd.org/fossil-fuels/publication/Indonesia%20G20%20Self-Report%20IFFS.pdf.

Metschies, G. P. 1999. *Fuel Prices and Taxation: Pricing Policies for Diesel, Fuel and Gasoline in Developing Countries and Global Motorization Data.* Frankfurt: Deutsche Gesellschaft für Technische Zusammenarbeit.

Mirzaee Ghazani, M. and M. Ali Jafari. 2021. The Efficiency of CO_2 Market in the Phase III EU ETS: Analyzing in the Context of a Dynamic Approach. *Environmental Science and Pollution Research.* 28. pp. 61080–61095. https://doi.org/10.1007/s11356-021-15044-5.

Nathan Associates. 2016. *Peer Review on Fossil Fuel Subsidy Reforms in the Philippines. Final Report.* Produced for the US-APEC Technical Assistance to Advance Regional Integration Project. https://www.slideshare.net/andreweil/apec-ffsr-peer-review-report-philippines-july-2016-final71416.

National Audit Office. 2007. *The Climate Change Levy and Climate Change Agreements.* London. https://www.nao.org.uk/wp-content/uploads/2012/11/climate_change_review.pdf.

NCCS. 2002. *Carbon Tax.* Singapore: National Climate Change Secretariat. https://www.nccs.gov.sg/singapores-climate-action/mitigation-efforts/carbontax/ (accessed 30 June 2023).

Organisation for Economic Co-operation and Development (OECD). *OECD Work on Support for Fossil Fuels.* Paris: OECD. https://www.oecd.org/fossil-fuels/methodology/.

———. 2002. *Implementing Environmental Fiscal Reform: Income Distribution and Sectoral Competitiveness Issues.* Proceedings of a Conference held in Berlin, Germany, 27 June. Paris: OECD. https://www.cbd.int/financial/fiscalenviron/several-fiscalreform-oecd.pdf.

———. 2010. *Taxation, Innovation and the Environment.* Paris: OECD.

———. 2013. *Analysing Energy Subsidies in the Countries of Eastern Europe, Caucasus and Central Asia.* Paris: OECD.

———. 2018. Effective Carbon Rates 2018: Pricing Carbon Emissions Through Taxes and Emissions Trading, Paris: OECD Publishing. https://doi.org/10.1787/9789264305304-en.

———. 2021. *OECD Companion to the Inventory of Support Measures for Fossil Fuels 2021.* Paris: OECD. https://doi.org/10.1787/e670c620-en.

Parry, I., S. Black, and J. Roaf. 2021. Proposal for an International Carbon Price Floor among Large Emitters. *IMF Staff Climate Note.* No. 2021/001, Washington, DC: International Monetary Fund. https://www.imf.org/en/Publications/staff-climate-notes/Issues/2021/06/15/Proposal-for-an-International-Carbon-Price-Floor-Among-Large-Emitters-460468.

Pearce, D. 1991. The Role of Carbon Taxes in Adjusting to Global Warming. *Economic Journal.* 101(407). pp. 938–948. https://doi.org/10.2307/2233865.

Pereira, A. M., R. M. Pereira, and P. G. Rodrigues. 2016. A New Carbon Tax in Portugal: A Missed Opportunity to Achieve the Triple Dividend? *Energy Policy.* 93. pp. 110–118. http://dx.doi.org/10.1016/j.enpol.2016.03.002.

Pinzón Téllez, J. 2019. *The Colombian Carbon Tax Overview.* National Planning Department of Colombia. https://globalndcconference.org/2019/.

PMR and CPLC. 2018. *Guide to Communicating Carbon Pricing.* Washington, DC: Partnership for Market Readiness and Carbon Pricing Leadership Coalition, World Bank. https://openknowledge.worldbank.org/handle/10986/30921.

PMR and ICAP. 2021. *Emissions Trading in Practice: A Handbook on Design and Implementation.* Second edition. Washington, DC: Partnership for Market Readiness and International Carbon Action Partnership, World Bank. https://openknowledge.worldbank.org/handle/10986/35413.

———. 2022. *Governance of Emissions Trading Systems.* Washington, DC: Partnership for Market Readiness and International Carbon Action Partnership, World Bank. https://openknowledge.worldbank.org/handle/10986/37213.

Quemin, S. and M. Pahle. 2022. Financials Threaten to Undermine the Functioning of Emissions Markets. *Nat. Clim. Chang.* https://doi.org/10.1038/s41558-022-01560-w (accessed 19 May 2023).

Radio New Zealand. 2021. *Marshall and Solomons Urge Carbon Tax for Shipping Industry.* 16 March. https://www.rnz.co.nz/international/pacific-news/438514/marshall-and-solomons-urge-carbon-tax-for-shipping-industry.

Raworth, K., S. Wykes, and S. Bass. 2014. Securing Social Justice in Green Economies: A Review and Ten Considerations for Policymakers. *IIED Issue Paper.* London: International Institute for Environment and Development. https://pubs.iied.org/16578iied.

Regional Greenhouse Gas Initiative. 2022. *Model Rule and MOU Versions.* New York: Regional Greenhouse Gas Initiative. https://www.rggi.org/index.php/program-overview-and-design/design-archive/mou-model-rule.

Rivers, N. and B. Schaufele. 2015. Salience of Carbon Taxes in the Gasoline Market. *Journal of Environmental Economics and Management.* 74. pp. 23–36. https://doi.org/10.1016/j.jeem.2015.07.002.

Sartori, M. P. 2021. *Uruguay's Path to a Carbon-Neutral Economy.* Dilogo Chino. 21 October.

Seixas, J. et al. 2017. *The Role of Electricity in the Decarbonization of the Portuguese Economy.* University of Lisbon. https://www.edp.com/es/node/15861.

Soocheol, L., H. Pollitt, and K. Ueta. 2012. An Assessment of Japanese Carbon Tax Reform Using the E3MG Econometric Model. *Scientific World Journal.* https://doi.org/10.1100/2012/835917.

Steenkamp, L. 2022. South Africa's Carbon Tax Rate Goes Up but Emitters Get More Time to Clean Up. *The Conversation.* https://theconversation.com/south-africas-carbon-tax-rate-goes-up-but-emitters-get-more-time-to-clean-up-177834#:~:text=Treasury%20acknowledged%20that%20this%20rate,by%20the%20end%20of%202021.

Surtidores.uy. 2022. *El Impuesto al CO$_2$ Alcanzaría los 800 Millones de Pesos en el Primer mes de Recaudación* (The CO$_2$ tax would reach 800 million pesos in the first month of collection). 10 February. https://surtidores.uy/el-impuesto-al-co2-alcanzaria-los-800-millones-de-pesos-en-el-primer-mes-de-recaudacion/.

TNP2K. Tim Nasional Percepatan Penanggulangan Kemiskinanhttps (National Team for the Acceleration of Poverty Reduction). http://www.tnp2k.go.id/program/at-a-glance.

Tol, R. S. J. et al. 2008. A Carbon Tax for Ireland. *ESRI Working Paper.* No. 246, Dublin: Economic and Social Research Institute. http://hdl.handle.net/10419/50164.

Twidale, S. 2022. *Global Carbon Pricing Schemes Raised $84 Bln in 2021—World Bank.* Reuters. 24 May. https://jp.reuters.com/article/climate-change-carbon-pricing-idAFL5N2XG42A.

United Nations. 2001. *United Nations Handbook on Carbon Taxation for Developing Countries.* https://www.un.org/development/desa/financing/document/un-handbook-carbon-taxation-developing-countries-2021.

———. 2022. SDG Indicators: Global Indicator Framework for the Sustainable Development Goals and Targets of the 2030 Agenda for Sustainable Development, including Annual Refinements. https://unstats.un.org/sdgs/indicators/indicators-list/.

United Nations Climate Change[a]. GHG Data from UNFCCC. https://unfccc.int/process-and-meetings/transparency-and-reporting/greenhouse-gas-data/ghg-data-unfccc/ghg-data-from-unfccc (accessed 19 May 2023).

United Nations Climate Change[b]. IFI TWG—List of Methodologies. https://unfccc.int/climate-action/sectoral-engagement/ifis-harmonization-of-standards-for-ghg-accounting/ifi-twg-list-of-methodologies.

United Nations Environment Programme. 2019. *Measuring Fossil Fuel Subsidies in the Context of the Sustainable Development Goals*. Nairobi: United Nations Environment Programme. https://wedocs.unep.org/bitstream/handle/20.500.11822/28111/FossilFuel.pdf?sequence=1&isAllowed=y.

United Nations Framework Convention on Climate Change. 2022. The Glasgow Climate Pact—Decision 1/CMA.3. https://unfccc.int/sites/default/files/resource/cma2021_10_add1_adv.pdf.

Villanueva, J. 2021. *PH Moves to Institutionalize Carbon Pricing Instrument.* Philippine News Agency. 27 October. https://www.pna.gov.ph/articles/1157995.

Whitley, S. and L. van der Burg. 2015. *Fossil Fuel Subsidy Reform in Sub-Saharan Africa: From Rhetoric to Reality*. London and Washington, DC: New Climate Economy. http://newclimateeconomy.report/misc/working-papers.

———. 2018. Reforming Fossil Fuel Subsidies: The Art of the Possible. In J. Skovgaard and H. van Asselt, eds. *The Politics of Fossil Fuel Subsidies and Their Reform*. Cambridge University Press.

World Bank. 2022. Carbon Pricing Dashboard. https://carbonpricingdashboard.worldbank.org/map_data.

———. 2022. *State and Trends of Carbon Pricing 2022*. Washington, DC: World Bank. https://openknowledge.worldbank.org/handle/10986/37455.

World Health Organization. 2022. *Air Pollution*. Geneva: World Health Organization. https://www.who.int/health-topics/air-pollution#tab=tab_1.

Yong, S. 2021. Tax and Malaysia's Carbon Neutrality Ambition. *The Star*. 14 October.

www.ingramcontent.com/pod-product-compliance
Lightning Source LLC
Chambersburg PA
CBHW050049220326
41599CB00045B/7340